Copyright © 2011 by PAGODA Academy, Inc.

All rights reserved. No part of this publication may be reproduced, stored in a retrieval system, or transmitted, in any form, or by any means, electronic, mechanical, photocopying, recording or otherwise, without the prior written permission of the copyright holder and the publisher.

Published by PAGODA Books
PAGODA Books is the professional language publishing company of the PAGODA Education Group.
19F, PAGODA Tower, 419, Gangnam-daero,
Seocho-gu, Seoul, 06614, Rep. of KOREA
www.pagodabook.com

First published 2011
Twenty-seventh impression 2025
Printed in the Republic of Korea

ISBN 978-89-6281-243-5 (14740)

Publisher | Kyung-Sil Park
Writer | PAGODA Language Education Center
Illustrator | Eunhae Jeon, Nockjin Sung

Acknowledgements
Thanks to the following for their contributions in providing us feedback:
Hee Choi, Sunny Kwon, Hyun-Kyoung Kim, Mia Kim, Cindy Jung, James Kwak, Amy Lee, Lena Lee, Shin-Ok Won, Sooji Park, Rachel Shin, Joanne Lee, Jessie Lee, Maria Hong, Elisa Lee, Josephine Kim, Daniel Lee, Alvin Burch

A defective book may be exchanged at the store where you purchased it.

Introduction

i Can Speak **1 Red**, the first level of the *i* Can Speak series, is a speaking-focused course book for English learners who are at a very basic level. This book gives learners the opportunity to understand the basics of the English structure and become familiar with beginner-level vocabulary and basic expressions. This book also enables students to build up a strong foundation in the fundamentals of conversational English while developing their grammar skills at the same time.

There are 18 lessons in this book and each lesson consists of the following sections:

Warm-Up

This section introduces relevant vocabulary and expressions for each lesson through simple activities. This section provides a useful list of new words for beginners. As the lessons proceed, learners will be able to effectively preview the appropriate lexical items for a particular English conversation.

Dialogue

This section covers target sentences in authentic conversations between two people. It also helps listening skills and creates interest in the lesson by using role-play.

Grammar Point

This section provides the target structures of English for each lesson. This section helps students understand the grammatical forms and functions that are needed to convey meaning accurately.

Practice

This section provides practice drills that make use of the new dialogues using the given words or expressions. This controlled activity allows learners to become familiar with the dialogues using the target structures.

Pair Work

This section offers pair-work activity. It stimulates learners to use the information from the lesson to answer questions with peers.

Pronunciation

This section provides students with comparison work composed of often-confused sounds. This section can be applied in various ways; students can either simply listen and repeat the sentences or they can work in pairs and practice together.

*This course book is used best in collaboration with the on-line program.

Scope and Sequence

Introduction ———————————— 3
Pronunciation ———————————— 6
Have Fun with Tongue Twisters ———— 7
Classroom Language ———————— 8-9

	Topic	Grammar	Page
Lesson 01 I'm from Korea.	Countries, Nationalities	***Be verb:*** Contractions of Be verb Affirmative Statements	10
Lesson 02 Are you a doctor?	Occupations I	***Be verb:*** Negative Statements Yes/No Questions	16
Lesson 03 Who is she?	Family	***Be verb:*** Possessive Adjectives / Nouns Wh-Questions (Who)	22
Lesson 04 What is this?	Names of things I	***Singular / Plural Nouns:*** Yes/No Questions Wh-Questions (What)	28
Lesson 05 Whose car is it?	Names of things II	***Possessive Pronouns:*** Yes/No Questions Wh-Questions (Whose)	34
Lesson 06 Is there a TV in your bedroom?	Household items	***There is (are) / Is (Are) there~ ?*** Affirmative Statements Negative Statements Yes/No Questions Wh-Questions (What)	40
Lesson 07 Where is my wallet?	Locations of objects	***Prepositions of Place:*** Yes/No Questions Wh-Questions (Where)	46
Lesson 08 What time is the party?	Dates, Days, Time	***Impersonal Pronoun 'it':*** Wh-Questions (What, When)	52
Lesson 09 I get up at 7 every morning.	Daily routines	***Simple Present:*** Affirmative Statements Negative Statements Yes/No Questions Wh-Questions	60

	Topic	Grammar	Page
Lesson 10 **What do you do?**	Occupations II	**Simple Present:** Wh-Questions (What, Where)	**68**
Lesson 11 **I'm doing my homework.**	Current activities I	**Present Progressive:** Affirmative Statements Negative Statements Yes/No Questions	**74**
Lesson 12 **What are you doing?**	Current activities II	**Present Progressive:** Wh-Questions (What)	**80**
Lesson 13 **I can play tennis.**	Abilities, Sports	**Can** (for ability) Affirmative Statements Negative Statements Questions	**86**
Lesson 14 **Could you turn off the TV?**	Making requests	**Can, Could** (for request) Making Requests Accepting / Refusing	**92**
Lesson 15 **Is there any milk?**	Food items	**Countable / Uncountable Nouns** Singular / Plural Quantifiers	**98**
Lesson 16 **I was tired this morning.**	Physical states, Emotions	**Simple Past of Be verb:** Affirmative Statements Negative Statements Yes/No Questions	**104**
Lesson 17 **Where were you this morning?**	Past events I	**Simple Past of Be verb:** Wh-Questions (Where, Who)	**110**
Lesson 18 **What were you doing at 10 o'clock last night?**	Past events II	**Past Progressive:** Wh-Questions (What) Yes/No Questions	**116**

Pronunciation

b, v	b: **b**anana, **b**edroom, **b**rother
	v: **v**iolin, ner**v**ous, **v**ictory

l, r	l: **l**ead, **l**ight, p**l**ay
	r: **r**ead, **r**ight, p**r**ay

g, k	g: **g**ame, **g**uitar, **g**reat
	k: **k**itchen, **K**orea, the United **K**ingdom

f, p	f: **f**ight, **F**rench, **F**riday
	p: **p**lay, **p**aint, **p**ark

s, th	s: **s**inging, **s**kiing, **s**on
	th: **th**inking, **th**ree, bir**th**day

ch, sh	ch: **Ch**ina, wat**ch**, handker**ch**ief
	sh: hairbru**sh**, book**sh**elf, **sh**out

i, ea, ee	i: l**i**sten, s**i**t, s**i**ng
	ea: r**ea**d, b**ea**ch, t**ea**cher
	ee: sl**ee**ping, w**ee**kend

Have Fun with Tongue Twisters

Peter Piper picked a peck of pickled peppers.

Shy Shelly says she shall sew sheets.

Which witch wished which wicked wish?

A big black bear sat on a big black bug.

Red lolly, yellow lolly, red lolly, yellow lolly

Feathered fairy flutters and flies to Florida.

The thirty-three thieves thought that they thrilled the throne throughout Thursday.

I wish to wish the wish you wish to wish, but if you wish the wish the witch wishes, I won't wish the wish you wish to wish.

Classroom Language

Teacher's Talk

Students' Talk

Lesson 1
I'm from Korea.

Warm-Up *Match the correct words from the list to fill in the blanks.*

– Word List –

Japan	China	British	Germany
French	Spanish	Australian	Korean
the United States	Italy	Brazilian	Canada

Country: Korea
Nationality:

Canadian

France

American

Country: the United Kingdom
Nationality:

Chinese

Australia

Italian

Country:
Nationality: German

Japanese

Brazil

Spain

Dialogue — Listen to the dialogue and practice.

John: Hello, I'm John Smith.
Nicole: Hi, my name is Nicole Dalion. *Where are you from?*
John: *I'm from the United States. What nationality are you?*
Nicole: *I'm Spanish.*
John: Oh, I see. Nice to meet you.
Nicole: Nice to meet you, too.

Comprehension Check!
Where is the man from? | What nationality is the woman?

Role-Play
Using the above dialogue, roleplay with your partner using your own personal information.

Grammar Point 1 — Contractions of Be verb

Singular Form	Contractions	Plural Form	Contractions
I **am**	= I**'m**	We **are**	= We**'re**
You **are**	= You**'re**	You **are**	= You**'re**
He **is**	= He**'s**	They **are**	= They**'re**
She **is**	= She**'s**		

Lesson 1 · 11

Grammar Point 2 To Be: Affirmative Statements

I am from Australia.	**I'm** Australian.
You are from Germany.	**You're** German.
He / She is from America.	**He / She's** American.
We are from Italy.	**We're** Italian.
You are from the United Kingdom.	**You're** British.
They are from Korea.	**They're** Korean.

Practice Practice the dialogue with a partner. See the example below.

you
France / French

Example

A: Where **are you** from?
B: **I'm** from **France**.
A: Oh, **you're French**.
   I'm **French**, too.

1
he
the United States / American

2
she
Spain / Spanish

3
they
Japan / Japanese

4
they
Italy / Italian

5
he
Germany / German

6
you
Korea / Korean

i Can Speak **1 Red** 12

Pair Work

STUDENT A

Divide the class into pairs. One student will be **Student A**, and the other will be **Student B**. Referring to the sample dialogue below, form questions and answers using the information provided.

You are ...
- Name: Jung
- Country: Korea
- Nationality: Korean

Your partner is ...
- Name: Robert
- Country: the UK (=England)
- Nationality: British

☺ : Hello, I'm <u>Jung</u>. What's your name?
☺ : I'm <u>Robert</u>.
☺ : How do you spell your name?
☺ : It's <u>R-O-B-E-R-T</u>. How about you?
☺ : It's <u>J-U-N-G</u>. Where are you from, <u>Robert</u>?
☺ : I'm from <u>the UK</u>.
☺ : Oh, then you are <u>British</u>, right?
☺ : Yeah, that's right. What nationality are you?
☺ : I'm <u>Korean</u>.
☺ : I see. You must be from <u>Korea</u>.

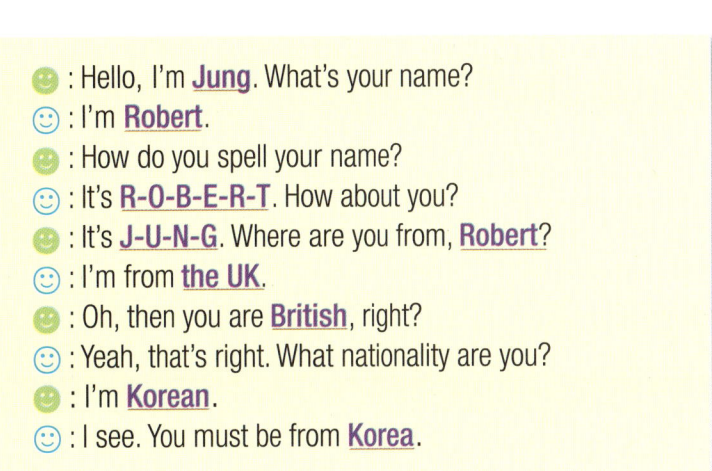

You are ...

	1	2	3
Name	Sophie	Carlos	Akiko
Country	France	Brazil	Japan
Nationality	French	Brazilian	Japanese

Your partner is ...

Name			
Country			
Nationality			

Lesson 1 · 13

Pair Work

Divide the class into pairs. One student will be **Student A**, and the other will be **Student B**. Referring to the sample dialogue below, form questions and answers using the information provided.

You are ...

Name:	Jung
Country:	Korea
Nationality:	Korean

Your partner is ...

Name:	Robert
Country:	the UK (=England)
Nationality:	British

☺ : Hello, I'm <u>Jung</u>. What's your name?
☺ : I'm <u>Robert</u>.
☺ : How do you spell your name?
☺ : It's <u>R-O-B-E-R-T</u>. How about you?
☺ : It's <u>J-U-N-G</u>. Where are you from, <u>Robert</u>?
☺ : I'm from <u>the UK</u>.
☺ : Oh, then you are <u>British</u>, right?
☺ : Yeah, that's right. What nationality are you?
☺ : I'm <u>Korean</u>.
☺ : I see. You must be from <u>Korea</u>.

You are ...

❶
Name: Paul
Country: Canada
Nationality: Canadian

❷
Name: Frank
Country: Germany
Nationality: German

❸
Name: Ming
Country: China
Nationality: Chinese

Your partner is ...

Name:
Country:
Nationality:

Pronunciation
Listen to the following sentences and repeat after them.

1. I am from Canada.
   I'm from Canada.

2. You are from Japan.
   You're from Japan.

3. We are from the United States.
   We're from the United States.

4. She is Spanish.
   She's Spanish.

5. He is Brazilian.
   He's Brazilian.

6. They are British.
   They're British.

Stretch Out!
Extra Questions

- What is the traditional food in your country?
- What are the popular places in your country?
- What is your favorite music?
- What is your favorite food?

Lesson 2
Are you a doctor?

Warm-Up Match the correct words from the list to complete the sentences.

– Word List –
flight attendant	chefs	doctors	photographer
pilot	fire fighter	teacher	lawyer
accountant	pharmacists	reporter	nurse

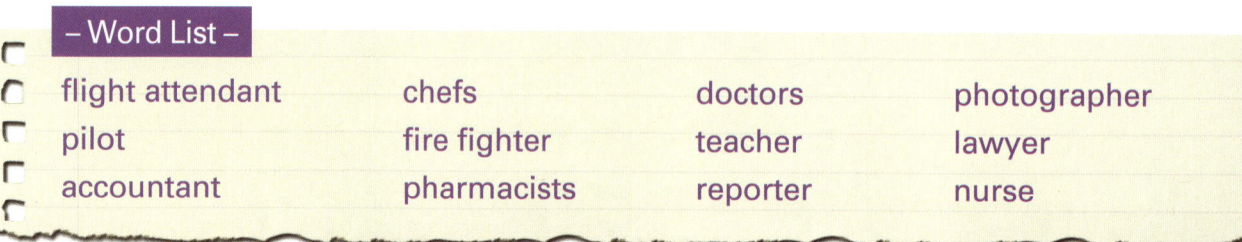

I'm a    You're a    She's a    She's a

I'm a

We're

They're   I'm a

He's an

You're a

I'm a

They're

Dialogue

Listen to the dialogue and practice.

Ted: Excuse me. **Are you Susie Miller?**
Susie: **Yes, I am.**
Ted: Hey, Susie. I'm Ted Kelly from 8th grade. Do you remember me?
Susie: Oh, Ted! Of course I remember you. **Are you a doctor?**
Ted: Oh, no, **I'm not. I'm a pharmacist.** I work in this hospital.
Susie: I see. It's great to see you again.

Comprehension Check!
Is Ted a doctor? | Is Ted a pharmacist? | Where does Ted work?

Role-Play
Using the above dialogue, roleplay with your partner using your own personal information.

Grammar Point 1 — To Be: Negative Statements

Affirmative Statements	Negative Statements	Negative Contractions
I **am** a doctor.	I **am not** a doctor.	I**'m not** a doctor.
You **are** a lawyer.	You **are not** a lawyer.	You**'re not** a lawyer. (= You **aren't** a lawyer.)
He/She **is** a chef.	He/She **is not** a chef.	He/She**'s not** a chef. (= He/She **isn't** a chef.)
We / You / They **are** teachers.	We / You / They **are not** teachers.	We / You / They**'re not** teachers. (= We / You / They **aren't** teachers.)

Lesson 2 · 17

Grammar Point 2 — To Be: Yes/No Questions

Yes/No Questions	Short Answers	
Am I a doctor?	Yes, you are.	No, you're not. (= No, you aren't.)
Are you a lawyer?	Yes, I am.	No, I'm not.
Is he/she a chef?	Yes, he/she is.	No, he/she's not. (= No, he/she isn't.)
Are we doctors?	Yes, you are.	No, you're not. (= No, you aren't.)
Are you lawyers?	Yes, we are.	No, we're not. (= No, we aren't.)
Are they chefs?	Yes, they are.	No, they're not. (= No, they aren't.)

Practice
Practice the dialogue with a partner. See the example below.

Ted Miller / Canada / British
a pilot / a flight attendant

Example

A: Are you Ted Miller?
B: Yes, I am.
A: Are you from Canada?
B: No, I'm not. I'm British.
A: Are you a pilot?
B: No, I'm not. I'm a flight attendant.

❶
Carlos / Brazil / Mexican
a reporter / a fire fighter

❷
Mrs. Wells / Spain
American / a pharmacist / a doctor

❸
Betty and Lisa / England
Australian / lawyers / nurses

❹
Nicole and Tom / France
Italian / nurses / chefs

❺
Sophia / Japan / Korean
an accountant / a pharmacist

❻
James / Germany / French
a doctor / a pilot

Pair Work

STUDENT A

Divide the class into pairs. One student will be *Student A,* and the other will be *Student B.* Referring to the sample dialogue below, form questions and answers using the information provided.

- ☺ : Is <u>he John</u>?
- ☺ : Is <u>he French</u>?
- ☺ : Is <u>he a flight attendant</u>?
- ☺ : Oh, I see. Is <u>he married</u>?

- ☺ : Yes, <u>he</u> is. / No, <u>he</u> isn't. <u>He is Tom</u>.
- ☺ : Yes, <u>he</u> is. / No, <u>he</u> isn't. <u>He's Spanish</u>.
- ☺ : Yes, <u>he</u> is. / No, <u>he</u> isn't. <u>He's a pilot</u>.
- ☺ : Yes, <u>he</u> is. / No, <u>he</u> isn't. <u>He's single</u>.

1 Ask *Student B* questions about the information in the chart. Check (✓) whether the information is true or false. If the information is false, write the correct answer.

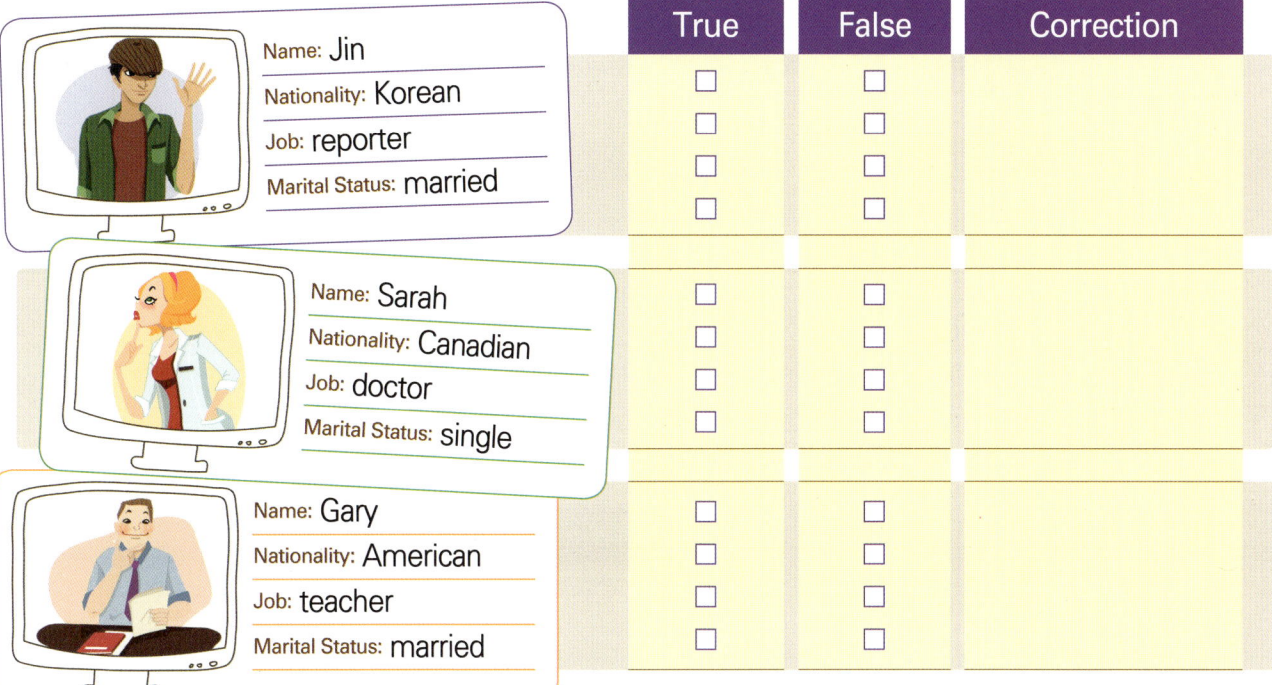

2 Answer *Student B*'s questions using the information about each person below.

Pair Work

STUDENT B

Divide the class into pairs. One student will be **Student A,** and the other will be **Student B**. Referring to the sample dialogue below, form questions and answers using the information provided.

- ☺ : Is <u>he John</u>?
- ☺ : Is <u>he French</u>?
- ☺ : Is <u>he a flight attendant</u>?
- ☺ : Oh, I see. Is <u>he married</u>?

- ☺ : Yes, <u>he</u> is. / No, <u>he</u> isn't. <u>He is Tom</u>.
- ☺ : Yes, <u>he</u> is. / No, <u>he</u> isn't. <u>He's Spanish</u>.
- ☺ : Yes, <u>he</u> is. / No, <u>he</u> isn't. <u>He's a pilot</u>.
- ☺ : Yes, <u>he</u> is. / No, <u>he</u> isn't. <u>He's single</u>.

1 Answer **Student A**'s questions using the information about each person below.

Name: Jin
Nationality: Japanese
Job: photographer
Marital Status: single

Name: Sue
Nationality: British
Job: pharmacist
Marital Status: single

Name: Gary
Nationality: German
Job: accountant
Marital Status: married

2 Ask **Student A** questions about the information in the chart. Check (✓) whether the information is true or false. If the information is false, write the correct answer.

	True	False	Correction
Name: Julie / Nationality: Spanish / Job: reporter / Marital Status: single	☐ ☐ ☐ ☐	☐ ☐ ☐ ☐	
Name: Brenda / Nationality: Canadian / Job: nurse / Marital Status: married	☐ ☐ ☐ ☐	☐ ☐ ☐ ☐	
Name: Paolo / Nationality: Brazilian / Job: fire fighter / Marital Status: married	☐ ☐ ☐ ☐	☐ ☐ ☐ ☐	

Pronunciation *Listen to the following sentences and repeat after them.*

1. You're not a chef.
   You aren't a chef.

2. She's not a pharmacist.
   She isn't a pharmacist.

3. He's not a fire fighter.
   He isn't a fire fighter.

4. They're not flight attendants.
   They aren't flight attendants.

5. Is he a lawyer?
   Is she a lawyer?

6. Are you reporters?
   Are they reporters?

7. Are you an accountant?
   Are you accountants?

Stretch Out!

List of Occupations

- athlete
- artist
- designer
- engineer
- editor
- consultant
- computer programmer
- investment banker
- model
- musician
- writer
- secretary
- salesman
- singer
- therapist
- housewife
- web designer
- veterinarian (=vet)

Lesson 2 · 21

Lesson 3

Who is she?

Warm-Up Referring to the family tree, match the correct words from the list below to complete the sentences.

– Word List –

grandfather	grandmother	husband	wife
father (dad)	mother (mom)	sister	brother
aunt	uncle	cousin	

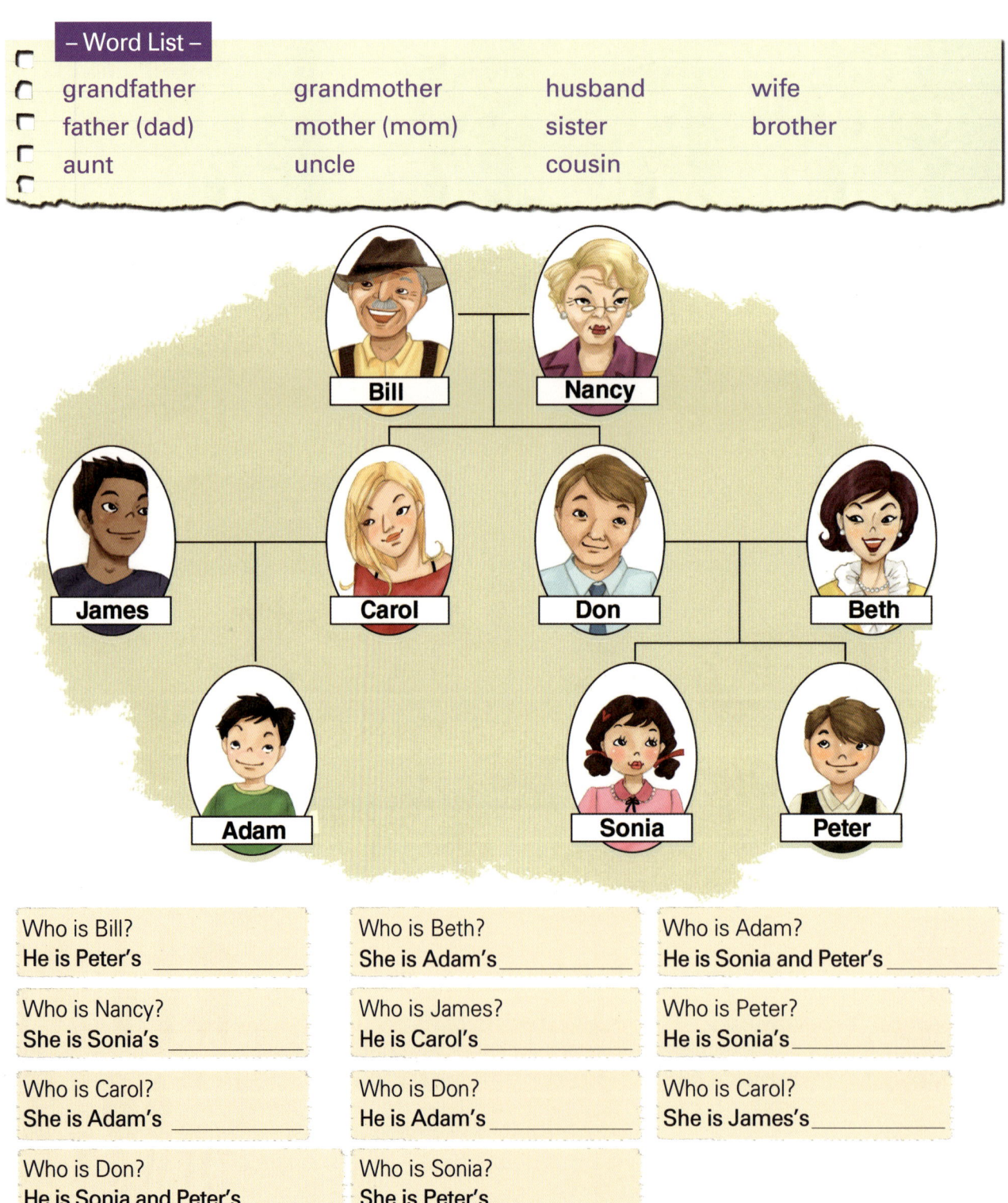

Who is Bill?
He is Peter's _____

Who is Beth?
She is Adam's _____

Who is Adam?
He is Sonia and Peter's _____

Who is Nancy?
She is Sonia's _____

Who is James?
He is Carol's _____

Who is Peter?
He is Sonia's _____

Who is Carol?
She is Adam's _____

Who is Don?
He is Adam's _____

Who is Carol?
She is James's _____

Who is Don?
He is Sonia and Peter's _____

Who is Sonia?
She is Peter's _____

Dialogue  Listen to the dialogue and practice.

Erin: Hello, Roy.
Roy: Hi, Erin.
Erin: *Is this your family picture?*
Roy: Yes, it is.
Erin: *Are they your parents?*
Roy: Yes, they are.
Erin: They look so happy. *And, who is he?*
Roy: *He is my brother.*
Erin: Wow! He is handsome. *What's his name?*
Roy: Andy.

Comprehension Check!
What are Erin and Roy looking at? | Who is Andy? | Is Andy handsome?

Role-Play
Using the above dialogue, roleplay with your partner using your own personal information.

Grammar Point 1 *Possessive Adjectives / Nouns*

	Subject Pronouns	Possessive Adjectives	Possessive Nouns
Singular	I	**my** picture	**Susan's** picture **my brother's** picture
Singular	You	**your** picture	**Susan's** picture **my brother's** picture
Singular	He	**his** picture	**Susan's** picture **my brother's** picture
Singular	She	**her** picture	**Susan's** picture **my brother's** picture
Singular	It	**its** picture	**Susan's** picture **my brother's** picture
Plural	You	**your** pictures	**children's** pictures **girls'** pictures
Plural	We	**our** pictures	**children's** pictures **girls'** pictures
Plural	They	**their** pictures	**children's** pictures **girls'** pictures

Grammar Point 2 — To Be: Wh-Questions (Who)

Wh-Questions	Answers
Who am I?	You're **Tom's** son.
Who are you?	I'm **his** uncle.
Who is he?	He's **my** brother.
Who is she?	She's **David's** sister.
Who are you?	We're **their** cousins.
Who are they?	They're **Fiona's** aunts.

Practice
Practice the dialogue with a partner. See the example below.

mom / Diane / a doctor

Example

A: Who <u>is she</u>?
B: <u>She's</u> my <u>mom</u>.
A: <u>What's her name</u>?
B: <u>Diane</u>.
A: <u>Is she a doctor</u>?
B: Yes, <u>she is</u>.

1. sister / Kelly / a lawyer

2. cousin / Andy / a photographer

3. dad / Mark / a fire fighter

4. grandparents / Richard and Jane / teachers

5. brother / Chris / a flight attendant

6. uncle and aunt / Joe and Wendy / accountants

Pair Work

STUDENT A

Divide the class into pairs. One student will be **Student A**, and the other will be **Student B**. Referring to the sample dialogue below, form questions and answers using the information provided.

😊 : Who is **Fred**?
☺ : **He's Ted's grandfather**.
😊 : Oh, I see. Is **he a police officer**?
☺ : **No, he isn't. He's a professor**.

Fred / police officer?

1 Ask **Student B** questions about Susan's family and complete the family tree.

John / pilot?   Andrew / chef?   Joanne / nurse?
Jane / teacher?   Jack / reporter?   Cathy / flight attendant?

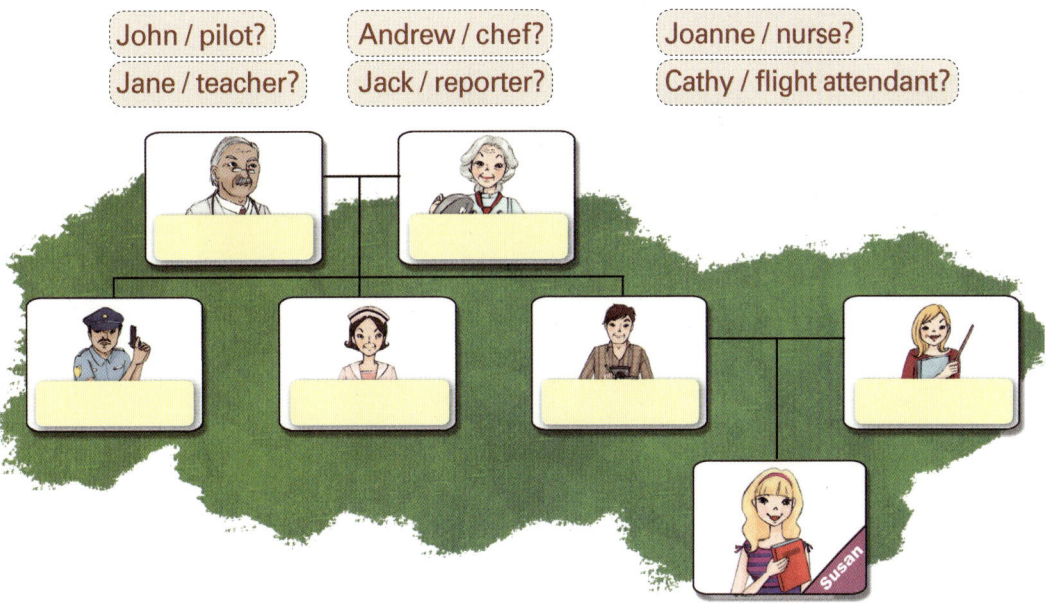

2 Answer **Student B**'s questions based on the information in Michael's family tree below.

Lesson 3 · 25

Pair Work

STUDENT B

Divide the class into pairs. One student will be **Student A,** and the other will be **Student B**. Referring to the sample dialogue below, form questions and answers using the information provided.

😊 : Who is <u>Fred</u>?
🙂 : <u>He's Ted's grandfather</u>.
😊 : Oh, I see. Is <u>he a police officer</u>?
🙂 : <u>No, he isn't. He's a professor</u>.

Fred / police officer?

1 Answer **Student A**'s questions based on the information in Susan's family tree below.

2 Ask **Student A** questions about Michael's family and complete the family tree.

Kevin / chef?   Diane / model?   Carol / teacher?
Ted / firefighter?   Paul / accountant?   David / pilot?

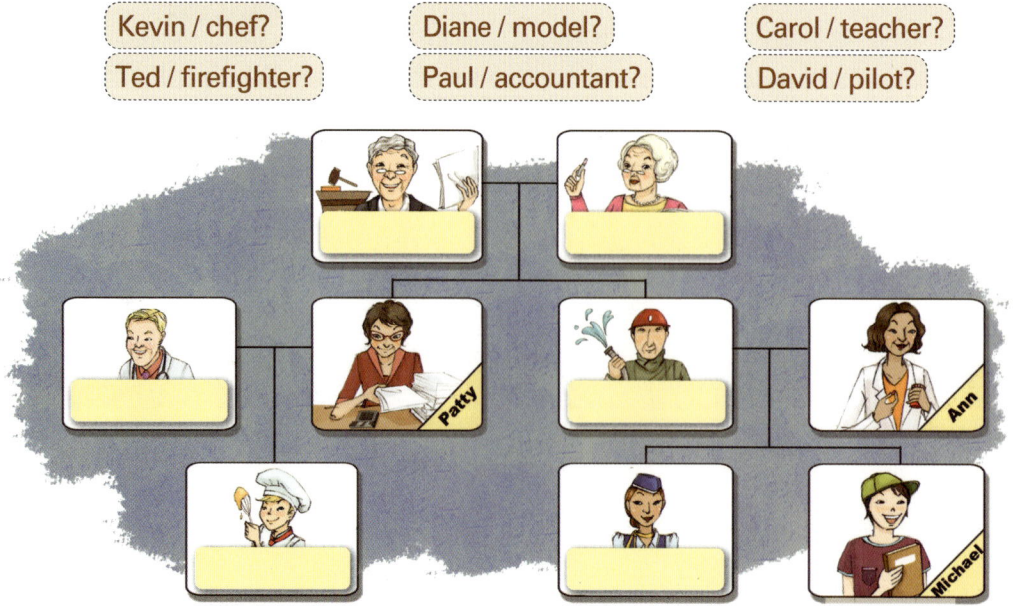

Pronunciation — Listen to the following sentences and repeat after them.

1. Robert is David's cousin.
   David is Robert's cousin.

2. Susan isn't Peter's grandmother.
   Peter isn't Susan's grandchild.

3. Is he Susie and Helen's grandfather?
   Are they Susie's and Helen's grandfathers?

4. Who is he?
   Who is she?

5. They are Fiona's parents.
   They're Fiona's parents.

Stretch Out!

Extra Questions on Relatives

- What do you call your <u>sister or brother's daughter</u>?
- What do you call your <u>sister or brother's son</u>?
- What do you call your <u>husband or wife's father</u>?
- What do you call your <u>husband or wife's mother</u>?
- What do you call your <u>husband or wife's sister</u>?
- What do you call your <u>husband or wife's brother</u>?

Lesson 4
What is this?

Warm-Up Match the words and pictures. Write the letter in the box of the corresponding picture.

– Word List –

- a. sunglasses
- b. shoes
- c. a wallet
- d. stockings
- e. a necklace
- f. cell phones
- g. a watch
- h. hairbrushes
- i. bow ties
- j. an mp3 player
- k. earrings
- l. gloves
- m. socks
- n. an umbrella
- o. boots
- p. handkerchiefs
- q. a briefcase
- r. a shoulder bag
- s. scarves
- t. rings

Dialogue  Listen to the dialogue and practice.

Cathy: Tom, *what's this? Is this a cell phone?*
Tom: *No, it isn't. It's an mp3 player.*
Cathy: Is this your mp3 player?
Tom: Yes, it is. Cathy, *what are these?*
Cathy: *They are earrings.*
Tom: *Are these your earrings?*
Cathy: *No, they aren't.* They are my sister's earrings.
Tom: Are they expensive?
Cathy: Yes, they are.

Comprehension Check!
What is this?  | What are these?

Role-Play
Using the above dialogue, roleplay with your partner using your own personal information.

Grammar Point 1 *Singular & Plural Nouns*

Rules	Singular Nouns	Plural Nouns
regular nouns ➔ **-s**	**a** necklace	necklace**s**
	an umbrella*	umbrella**s**
-s, -ch, -sh, -z, -x ➔ **-es**	**a** hairbrush	hairbrush**es**
	a watch	watch**es**
-f, -fe ➔ **-ves**	**a** scarf	scar**ves**
vowel + f ➔ **-s**	**a** handkerchief	handkerchief**s**
vowel + y ➔ **-s**	**a** key	key**s**

* **an**: is used with a noun that starts with vowel sound (/a/, /e/, /i/, /o/, /u/)
　(e.g.) a<u>n</u> <u>a</u>pple | a<u>n</u> <u>e</u>lephant | a<u>n</u> <u>m</u>p3 player | a<u>n</u> <u>o</u>range

Lesson 4 · 29

Grammar Point 2   To Be: Yes/No Questions, Wh-Questions (What)

	Singular		Plural	
Yes/No Questions	Is this **a key**? Yes, it is. / No, it isn't. Is that **a bag**? Yes, it is. / No, it isn't.		Are these **keys**? Yes, they are. / No, they aren't. Are those **bags**? Yes, they are. / No, they aren't.	
Wh-Questions (What)	What is this? What is that? What is it?	It's **a cap**. It's **a laptop**. It's **an mp3 player**.	What are these? What are those? What are they?	They're **earrings**. They're **gloves**. They're **sneakers**.

Practice   Practice the dialogue with a partner. See the example below.

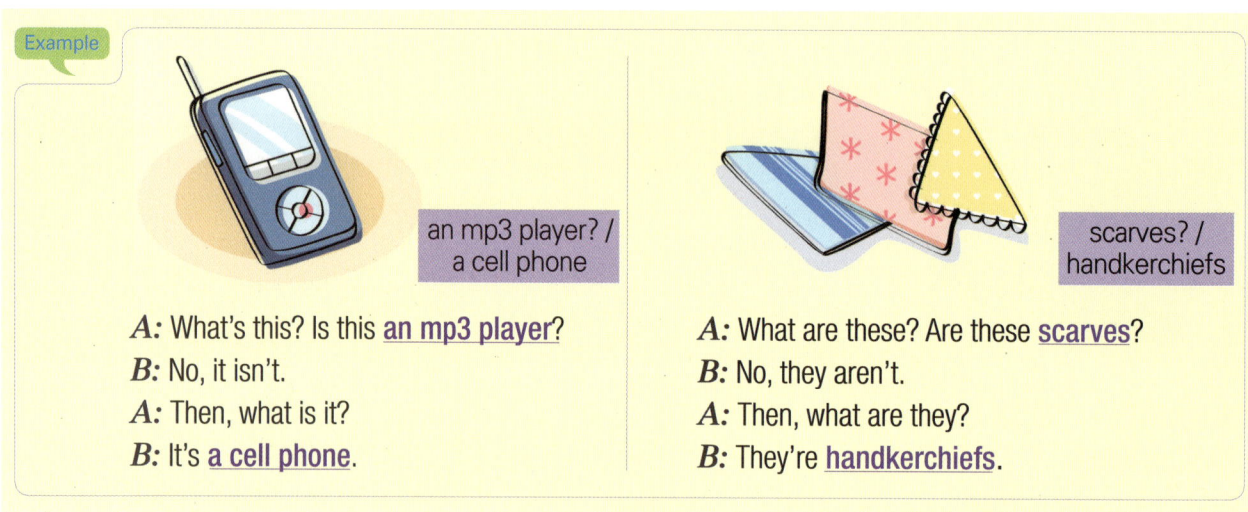

Example

an mp3 player? / a cell phone

A: What's this? Is this <u>an mp3 player</u>?
B: No, it isn't.
A: Then, what is it?
B: It's <u>a cell phone</u>.

scarves? / handkerchiefs

A: What are these? Are these <u>scarves</u>?
B: No, they aren't.
A: Then, what are they?
B: They're <u>handkerchiefs</u>.

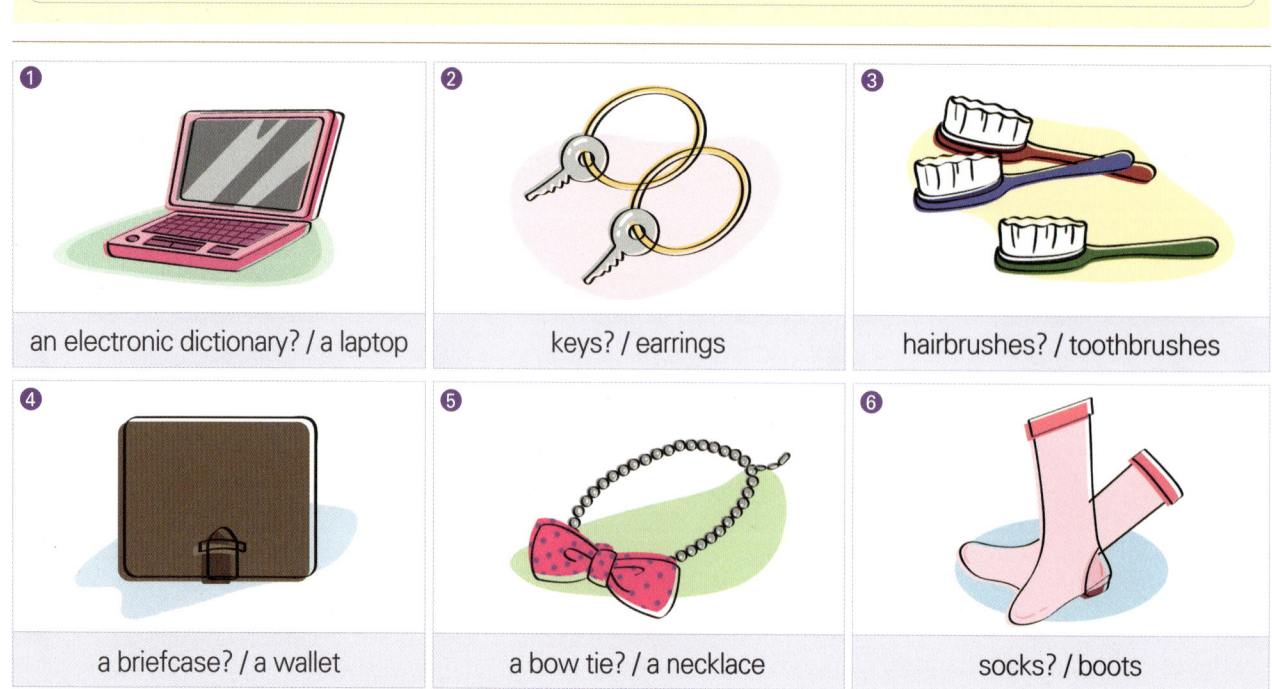

1. an electronic dictionary? / a laptop
2. keys? / earrings
3. hairbrushes? / toothbrushes
4. a briefcase? / a wallet
5. a bow tie? / a necklace
6. socks? / boots

Pair Work

STUDENT A

Divide the class into pairs. One student will be **Student A,** and the other will be **Student B**. Referring to the sample dialogue below, form questions and answers using the information provided.

- : Is this <u>Crystal's hat</u>?
- : Yes, it is............................ end
  No, it isn't........................ continue
- : Then, is this <u>Nicole's hat</u>?
- : Yes, it is. / No, it isn't.
- : Oh, then it must be <u>Adam's hat</u>.
- : That's right.

- : Are these <u>Crystal's hats</u>?
- : Yes, they are............................ end
  No, they aren't........................ continue
- : Then, are these <u>Nicole's hats</u>?
- : Yes, they are. / No, they aren't.
- : Oh, then they must be <u>Adam's hats</u>.
- : That's right.

1 Ask **Student B** questions to find out to whom each item belongs. Then write the names of the items in the correct box.

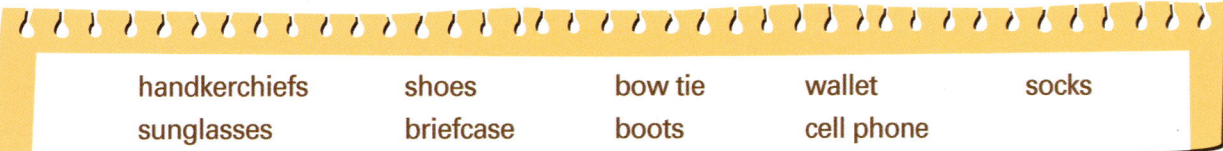

handkerchiefs   shoes   bow tie   wallet   socks
sunglasses   briefcase boots   cell phone

Crystal's belongings   Adam's belongings   Danny's belongings

2 Answer **Student B**'s questions based on the pictures below.

Helen's belongings

Robert's belongings

Nicole's belongings

Pair Work

STUDENT B

Divide the class into pairs. One student will be **Student A,** and the other will be **Student B**. Referring to the sample dialogue below, form questions and answers using the information provided.

☺ : Is this **Crystal's hat**?
☺ : Yes, it is. .... end
   No, it isn't. .... continue
☺ : Then, is this **Nicole's hat**?
☺ : Yes, it is. / No, it isn't.
☺ : Oh, then it must be **Adam's hat**.
☺ : That's right.

☺ : Are these **Crystal's hats**?
☺ : Yes, they are. .... end
   No, they aren't. .... continue
☺ : Then, are these **Nicole's hats**?
☺ : Yes, they are. / No, they aren't.
☺ : Oh, then they must be **Adam's hats**.
☺ : That's right.

1 Answer **Student A**'s questions based on the pictures below.

Crystal's belongings   Adam's belongings   Danny's belongings

2 Ask **Student A** questions to find out to whom each item belongs. Then write the names of the items in the correct box.

| necklace | watch | mp3 player | umbrella | shoulder bag |
| earrings | hairbrush | stockings | scarves | |

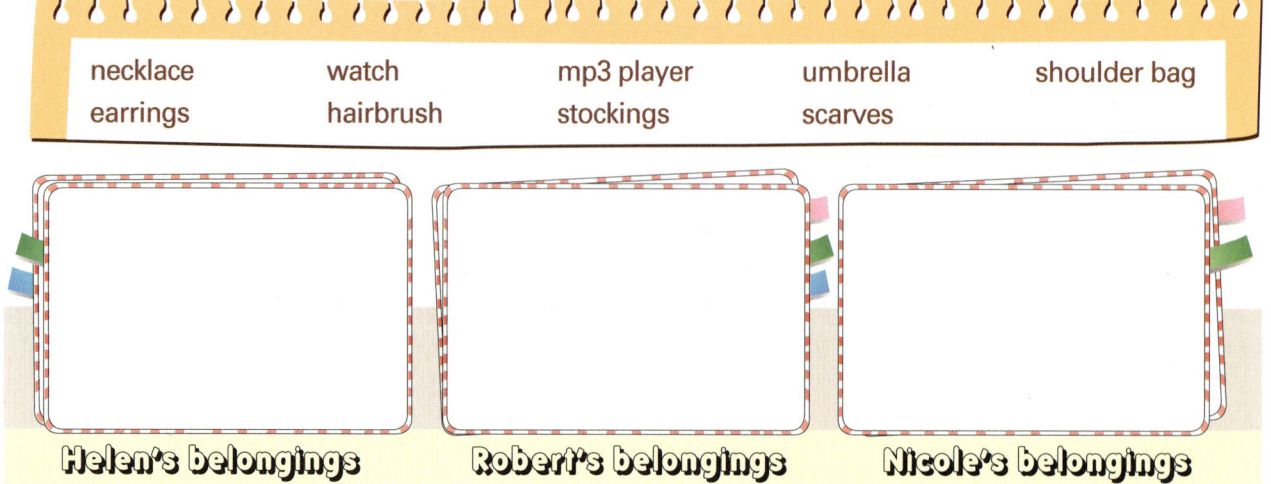

Helen's belongings   Robert's belongings   Nicole's belongings

Pronunciation
Listen to the following sentences and repeat after them.

1. It is a watch.
   They are watches.

2. It is a necklace.
   They are necklaces.

3. It's a handkerchief.
   They're handkerchiefs.

4. It's a toothbrush.
   They're toothbrushes.

5. It's an umbrella.
   They're umbrellas.

Stretch Out!

Pronunciation Rules

Rules	Examples	Pronunciation
–s → comes after p, k, t, f	caps books hats handkerchiefs	[s]
–s → comes after rest of the consonants	keys earrings bow ties	[z]
–es → comes after s, ch, sh, z, x	buses brushes churches watches boxes	[iz]

Lesson 5
Whose car is it?

Warm-Up Look at the picture below and match the words in the box to the appropriate category.

– Word List –

headset	suit	briefcase	jeans	heels
earrings	shoes	sunglasses	baseball cap	tie
cell phone	purse	watch	backpack	evening dress
rings	sneakers	T-shirt	necklace	

Ted's stuff

Cathy's stuff

Mark's stuff

Dialogue — Listen to the dialogue and practice.

Jane: Wow! Eric, *is this watch yours?*
Eric: No, *it's not mine.*
Jane: Then *whose watch is it?*
Eric: Hmm… I think *it's Tom's.*
Jane: Oh, really?
Eric: Yes, I think *it's his.*
Jane: I see. *Are those sneakers yours?*
Eric: *Yes, they are mine.*

Comprehension Check!

Whose watch is this?  | Whose sneakers are these?

Role-Play

Using the above dialogue, roleplay with your partner using your own personal information.

Grammar Point 1 — *Possessive Pronouns*

Subject Pronouns	Possessive Adjectives	Possessive Pronouns
I	my	**mine**
You	your	**yours**
He / She	his / her	**his / hers**
It	its	(x)
Susan	Susan's	**Susan's**
We	our	**ours**
They	their	**theirs**

Lesson 5 • 35

Grammar Point 2 To Be: Yes/No Questions, Wh-Questions (Whose)

	Singular	Plural
Yes/No Questions	Is this car **yours**? Yes, it is. / No, it isn't. Is that pencil **his**? Yes, it is. / No, it isn't.	Are these cars **yours**? Yes, they are. / No, they aren't. Are those pencils **his**? Yes, they are. / No, they aren't.
Wh-Questions (Whose)	Whose pencil is this? It's **mine**. (=It's my pencil.) Whose pen is that? It's **hers**. (=It's her pen.) Whose watch is it? It's **David's**. (=It's David's watch.)	Whose pencils are these? They're **his**. (=They're his pencils.) Whose pens are those? They're **theirs**. (=They're their pens.) Whose watches are they? They're **Kevin's and Eric's**. (=They're Kevin's and Eric's watches.)

Practice   Practice the dialogue with a partner. See the example below.

hat / mom sneakers

Example
A: Is this your **hat**?
B: No, it isn't. It's my **mom**'s.
A: Then, are those **sneakers** yours?
B: Yes, they are mine.

① necklace / sister / earrings

② briefcase / uncle / backpacks

③ purse / aunt / sunglasses

④ T-shirt / Alex / jeans

Pair Work

STUDENT A

Divide the class into pairs. One student will be **Student A,** and the other will be **Student B.** Referring to the sample dialogue below, form questions and answers using the information provided.

☺ : Wow! That <u>handkerchief</u> looks new. Is it yours?
☺ : No, it's not mine. (=No, it isn't mine.)
☺ : Then whose <u>handkerchief</u> is it?
☺ : It's <u>Crystal's</u>. I borrowed it from <u>her</u>.

☺ : Wow! Those <u>handkerchiefs</u> look new. Are they yours?
☺ : No, they're not mine. (=No, they aren't mine.)
☺ : Then whose <u>handkerchiefs</u> are they?
☺ : They're <u>Mark's</u>. I borrowed them from <u>him</u>.

1 Ask **Student B** questions to find out to whom each item belongs. Then write the names of the items in the correct box.

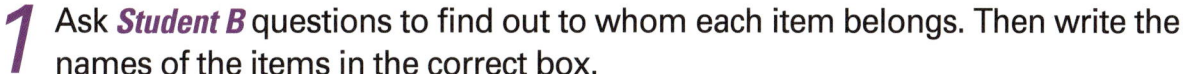

| watch | evening dress | gloves | necklace | boots | umbrella |
| ring | heels | sunglasses | earrings | shoulder bag | stockings |

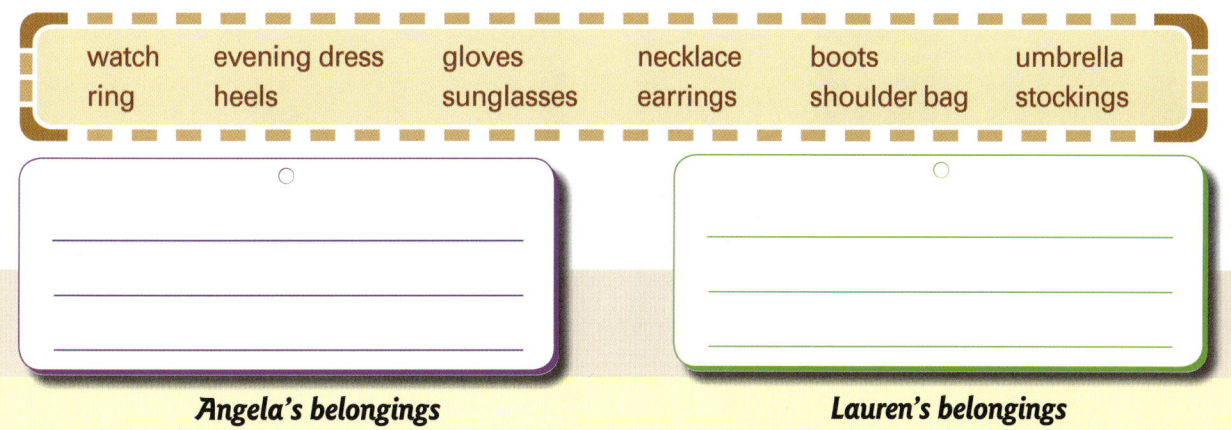

Angela's belongings   Lauren's belongings

2 Answer **Student B**'s questions based on the pictures below.

Peter   David

Lesson 5 · 37

Pair Work

STUDENT B

Divide the class into pairs. One student will be **Student A,** and the other will be **Student B.** Referring to the sample dialogue below, form questions and answers using the information provided.

- : Wow! That <u>handkerchief</u> looks new. Is it yours?
- : No, it's not mine. (=No, it isn't mine.)
- : Then whose <u>handkerchief</u> is it?
- : It's <u>Crystal's</u>. I borrowed it from <u>her</u>.

- : Wow! Those <u>handkerchiefs</u> look new. Are they yours?
- : No, they're not mine. (=No, they aren't mine.)
- : Then whose <u>handkerchiefs</u> are they?
- : They're <u>Mark's</u>. I borrowed them from <u>him</u>.

1 Answer **Student A**'s questions based on the pictures below.

Angela　　　　　　　　　　　　Lauren

2 Ask **Student A** questions to find out to whom each item belongs. Then write the names of the items in the correct box.

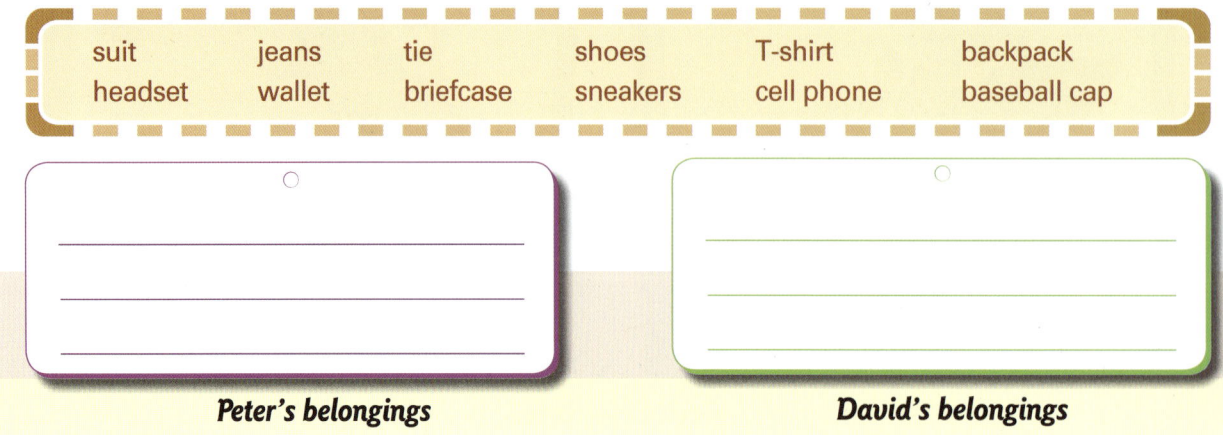

| suit | jeans | tie | shoes | T-shirt | backpack |
| headset | wallet | briefcase | sneakers | cell phone | baseball cap |

Peter's belongings　　　　　　　　　　David's belongings

Pronunciation Listen to the following sentences and repeat after them.

1 Is this cell phone yours?
Are these cell phones theirs?

2 Is that her watch?
Are those their watches?

3 Is this backpack mine?
Are these backpacks ours?

4 Whose cap is it?
Whose caps are they?

5 It's mine.
They're yours.

Stretch Out!

Common Items of Clothing

 a bow tie
 a skirt
 a vest
 a pair of glasses
 a pair of shorts
 a pullover
 a bracelet
 a pair of overalls
 flip-flops

Lesson 6 Is there a TV in your bedroom?

Warm-Up Look at the picture and match the number of each household item to its correct name.

Bedroom	Bathroom	Living room	Kitchen
☐ lamp	☐ toilet	☐ couches	☐ stove
☐ bed	☐ bathtub	☐ coffee table	☐ dishwasher
☐ desk	☐ bathroom sink	☐ treadmill	☐ refrigerator
☐ night table	☐ cabinet	☐ plants	☐ toaster
☐ dresser	☐ towels	☐ television	☐ microwave oven
☐ picture frames		☐ bookshelf	☐ dishes

Dialogue
Listen to the dialogue and practice.

Kevin: Tiffany, *is there a dishwasher in your kitchen?*
Tiffany: *Yes, there is.*
Kevin: What else is in your kitchen?
Tiffany: *There is a microwave oven, a stove and a refrigerator.*
Kevin: I see. *Is there a TV in your bedroom?*
Tiffany: *No, there isn't.* It's in the living room.

Comprehension Check!
Is there a refrigerator in Tiffany's kitchen? | Is there a TV in Tiffany's bedroom?

Role-Play
Using the above dialogue, roleplay with your partner using your own personal information.

Grammar Point 1   *There is / There are…*

	Singular	Plural
Affirmative Statement	**There is** a TV in the living room.	**There are** two couches in the living room.
Negative Statement	**There isn't** a TV in the living room. (= **There is no** TV in the living room.)	**There aren't** two couches in the living room. (= **There are no** couches in the living room.)
Yes/No Questions	**Is there** a TV in the living room? → Yes, there is. / No, there isn't.	**Are there** couches in the living room? → Yes, there are. / No, there aren't.

Lesson 6 · 41

Grammar Point 2 *Wh-Questions*

Wh-Questions	Answers
What is in your living room?	**There is** a treadmill and a coffee table in my living room. **There are** bookshelves and couches in my living room.

Practice
Practice the dialogue with a partner. See the example below.

Example

a couch / bedroom
living room

A: Is there a **couch** in your **bedroom**?
B: No, there isn't.
A: Then where is it?
B: It's in the **living room**.

plants / bedroom
living room

A: Are there **plants** in your **bedroom**?
B: No, there aren't.
A: Then where are they?
B: They're in the **living room**.

1. a lamp / living room
bedroom

2. a bookshelf / bedroom
living room

3. picture frames / bathroom
bedroom

4. towels / kitchen
bathroom

5. a television / bedroom
living room

6. dishes / bathroom
kitchen

Pair Work

STUDENT A

Divide the class into pairs. One student will be **Student A,** and the other will be **Student B.** Find out about the household items that **Student B** has that you don't have by asking each other questions. You can **only ask one question at a time** and **answer one item at a time**.

- 😊 : What is in your <u>living room</u>?
- 🙂 : There is <u>a couch</u> in my <u>living room</u>. / There are <u>couches</u> in my <u>living room</u>.
- 😊 : What else is in your <u>living room</u>?

  continue

◆ What household items does **Student B** have that you don't have?

Living room	Bedroom	Bathroom	Kitchen

Lesson 6 • 43

Pair Work

STUDENT B

Divide the class into pairs. One student will be **Student A,** and the other will be **Student B.** Find out about the household items that **Student A** has that you don't have by asking each other questions. You can **only ask one question at a time** and **answer one item at a time.**

☺ : What is in your living room?
☺ : There is a couch in my living room. / There are couches in my living room.
☺ : What else is in your living room?
   continue

◆ What household items does **Student A** have that you don't have?

Living room	Bedroom	Bathroom	Kitchen

Pronunciation

Listen to the following sentences and repeat after them.

1. What is in your **bathroom**?
   What is in your **bedroom**?

2. **There's** a bookshelf in the bedroom.
   There is a bookshelf in the bedroom.

3. **There is a dish** in the kitchen.
   There are dishes in the kitchen.

4. **Is there a couch** in your living room?
   Are there couches in your living room?

5. There **aren't any** towels in the bathroom.
   There **are many** towels in the bathroom.

Stretch Out!

Additional Rooms

▸ cloakroom	▸ dining room	▸ garage	▸ guest room

People put their clothes in the **cloakroom.**	People eat their food in the **dining room.**	People usually park their cars in the **garage.**	People such as friends or guests sleep in the **guest room.**

Lesson 7
Where is my wallet?

Warm-Up Fill in the blank for each picture using the word list below.

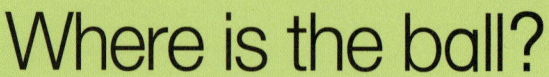

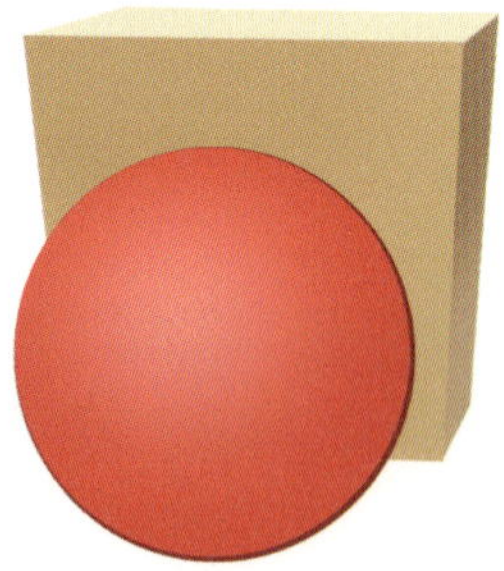

The ball is _____ the box.

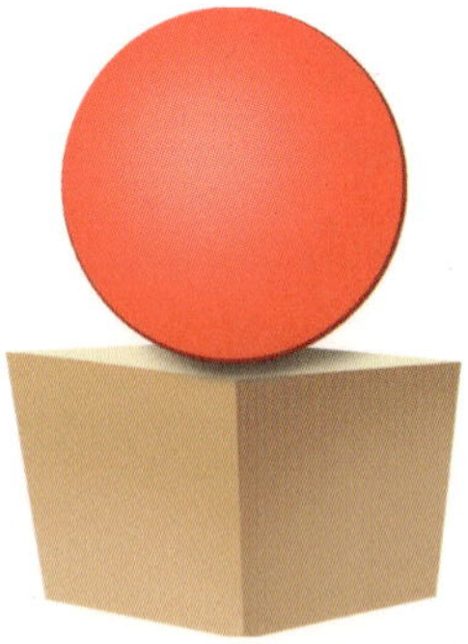

The ball is _____ the box.

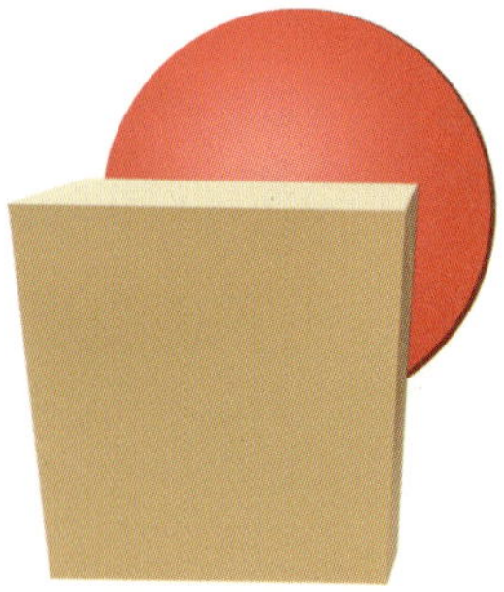

The ball is _____ the box.

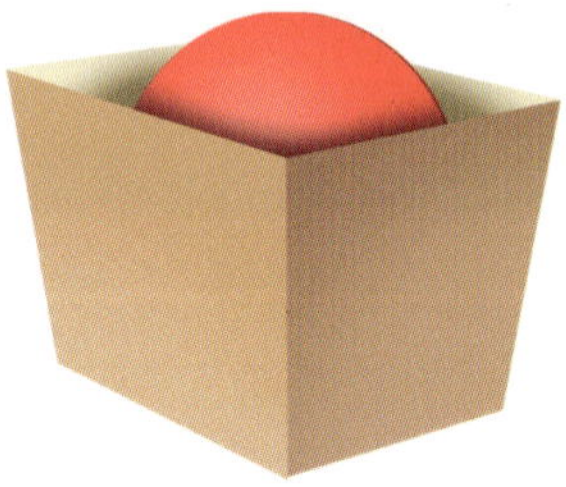

The ball is _____ the box.

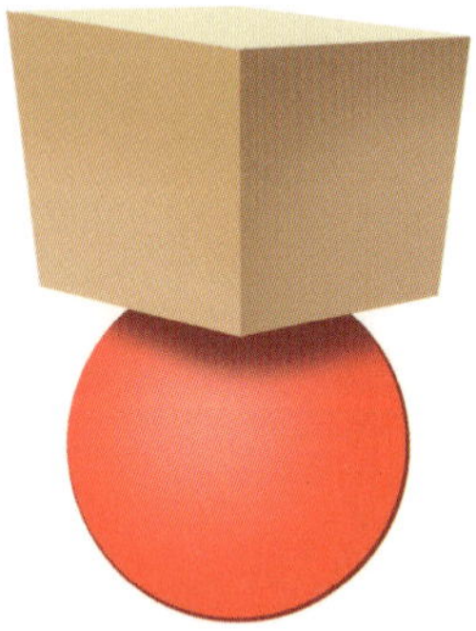

The ball is _____ the box.

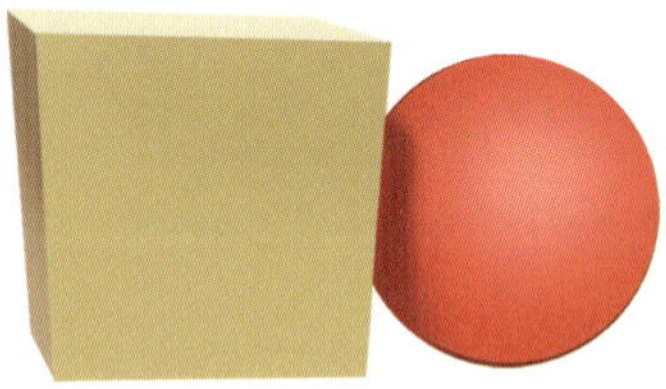

The ball is _____ the box.

– Word List –

in   on   under   next to   in front of   behind

Dialogue — Listen to the dialogue and practice.

Jack: Oh no! I'm late for work.
Wendy: Hurry up, Jack!
Jack: Okay okay. **Where is my wallet?**
Wendy: **It's on the chair.**
Jack: **Where are my socks?**
Wendy: **They're under the bed.**
Jack: **Where's my briefcase?**
Wendy: **It's next to the dresser.**
You'd better organize your room.

Comprehension Check!
Where is Jack's wallet? | Where are Jack's socks? | Where is Jack's briefcase?

Role-Play
Using the above dialogue, roleplay with your partner using your own personal information.

Grammar Point 1 — Prepositions of Place

 The ball is **in front of** the box.

 The ball is **on** the box.

 The ball is **behind** the box.

 The ball is **under** the box.

 The ball is **next to** the box.

 The ball is **in** the box.

Grammar Point 2 To Be: Yes/No Questions, Wh-Questions

	Singular	Plural
Yes/No Questions	Is the headset **on the table**? Yes, it is. No, it isn't. It's **under the table**.	Are the keys **in the box**? Yes, they are./No, they aren't. They're **next to the box**.
Wh-Questions (Where)	**Where** is my backpack? It's **behind the chair**.	**Where** are your glasses? They're **in front of the lamp**.

Practice Practice the dialogue with a partner. See the example below.

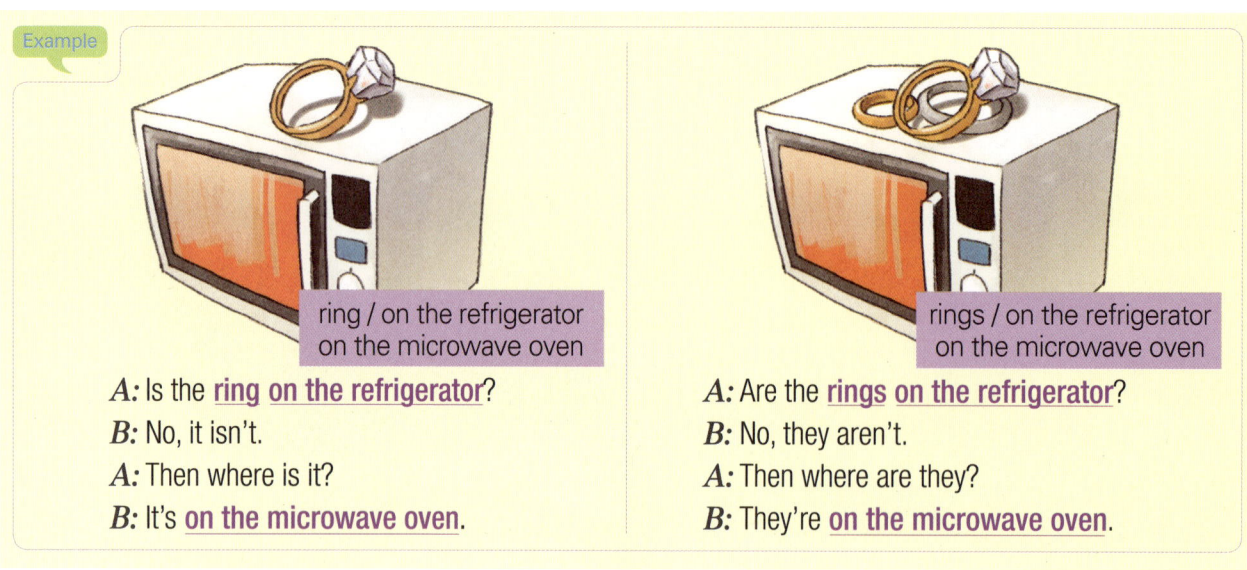

Example

ring / on the refrigerator
on the microwave oven

A: Is the ring on the refrigerator?
B: No, it isn't.
A: Then where is it?
B: It's on the microwave oven.

rings / on the refrigerator
on the microwave oven

A: Are the rings on the refrigerator?
B: No, they aren't.
A: Then where are they?
B: They're on the microwave oven.

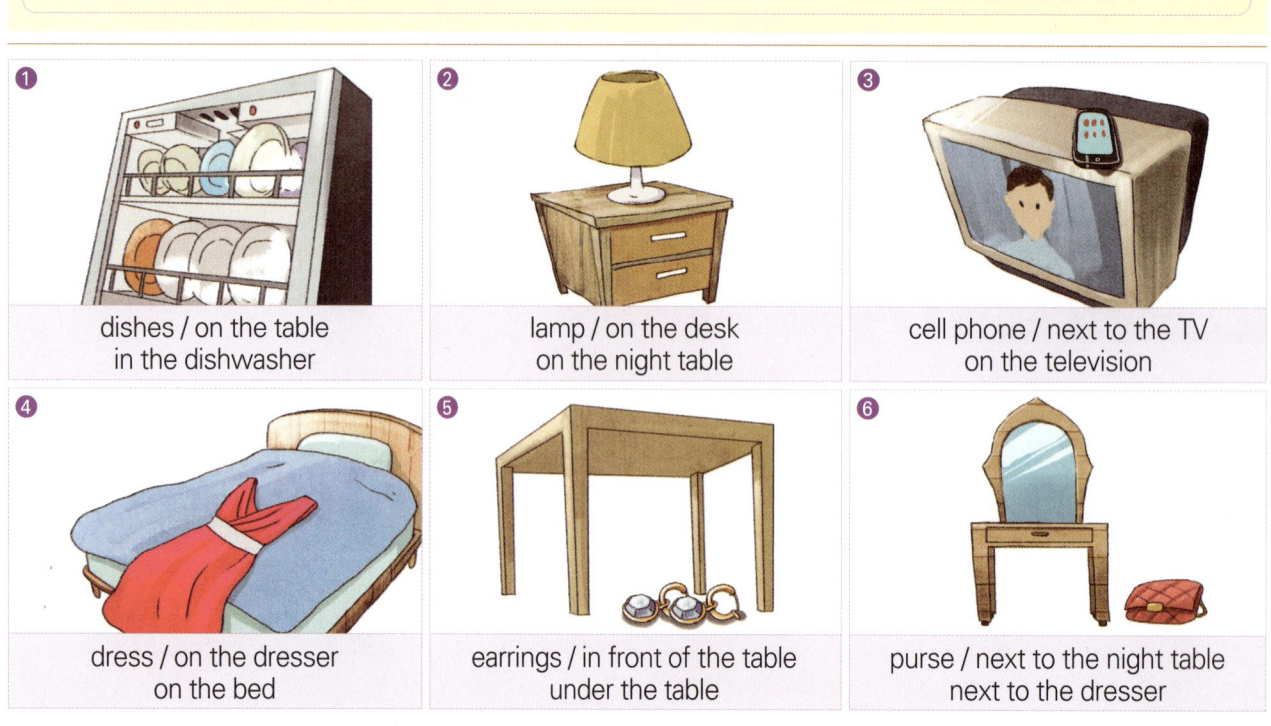

1. dishes / on the table / in the dishwasher
2. lamp / on the desk / on the night table
3. cell phone / next to the TV / on the television
4. dress / on the dresser / on the bed
5. earrings / in front of the table / under the table
6. purse / next to the night table / next to the dresser

Pair Work

STUDENT A

Divide the class into pairs. One student will be **Student A,** and the other will be **Student B.** Referring to the sample dialogue below, form questions and answers using the information provided.

> ☺ : Oh, no. I'm in a hurry now.
> ☺ : What's the matter?
> ☺ : I'm late for work / school. But, I can't find my <u>glasses</u>. Where <u>are they</u>?
> ☺ : <u>They're on the coffee table</u>. Hurry up!

1 Ask **Student B** questions to find out where each item is and then draw it in the picture below.

2 Answer **Student B**'s questions based on the picture on the right.

Lesson 7 · 49

Pair Work

Divide the class into pairs. One student will be **Student A,** and the other will be **Student B.** Referring to the sample dialogue below, form questions and answers using the information provided.

> 😊 : Oh, no. I'm in a hurry now.
> ☺ : What's the matter?
> 😊 : I'm late for work / school. But, I can't find my <u>glasses</u>. Where <u>are they</u>?
> ☺ : <u>They're on the coffee table</u>. Hurry up!

1 Answer **Student A**'s questions based on the picture on the right.

2 Ask **Student A** questions to find out where each item is and then draw it in the picture below.

Pronunciation

Listen to the following sentences and repeat after them.

1 Is the headset **on** the desk?
Is the headset **under** the desk?

2 Are your shoes **in** the box?
Are your shoes **on** the box?

3 The dogs are **behind** the couch.
The dogs are **next to** the couch.

4 The lamp is in front of the **night table**.
The lamp is in front of the **coffee table**.

5 The towels are **next to** the bathtub.
The towels are **in** the bathtub.

Stretch Out!

Extra Prepositions of Place

▶ Where is the ball?

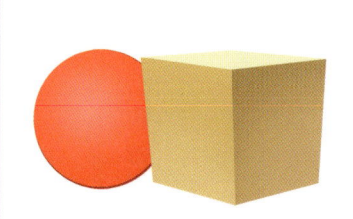

The ball is
on the left of the box.

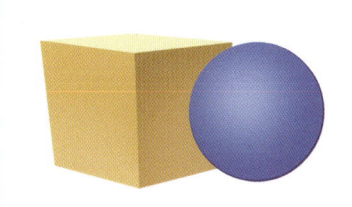

The ball is
on the right of the box.

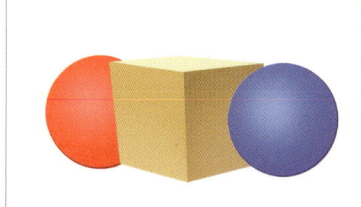

The box is **between** the
red ball **and** the blue ball.

Lesson 8

What time is the party?

Warm-Up

Match the correct months from the list to complete the chart.

May	September	July	March	November	~~January~~
August	December	April	October	~~June~~	February

Months of the Year

1 January	2	3	4	5
	6 June	7	8	9
	10	11	12	

◈ *Match the days and dates from the list to complete the calendar.*

- Thursday
- Tuesday
- Saturday
- Friday
- Monday

- eleventh
- fifteenth
- seventh
- twenty-second
- second
- thirtieth
- first
- nineteenth
- fourth
- twenty-seventh
- seventeenth
- twenty-third
- thirty-first
- twelfth
- third
- sixth
- twenty-eighth
- twenty-fourth
- twentieth

Sunday			Wednesday			
	1	2	3	4	5 fifth	6
7	8 eighth	9 ninth	10 tenth	11	12	13 thirteenth
14 fourteenth	15	16 sixteenth	17	18 eighteenth	19	20
21 twenty-first	22	23	24	25 twenty-fifth	26 twenty-sixth	27
28	29 twenty-ninth	30	31			

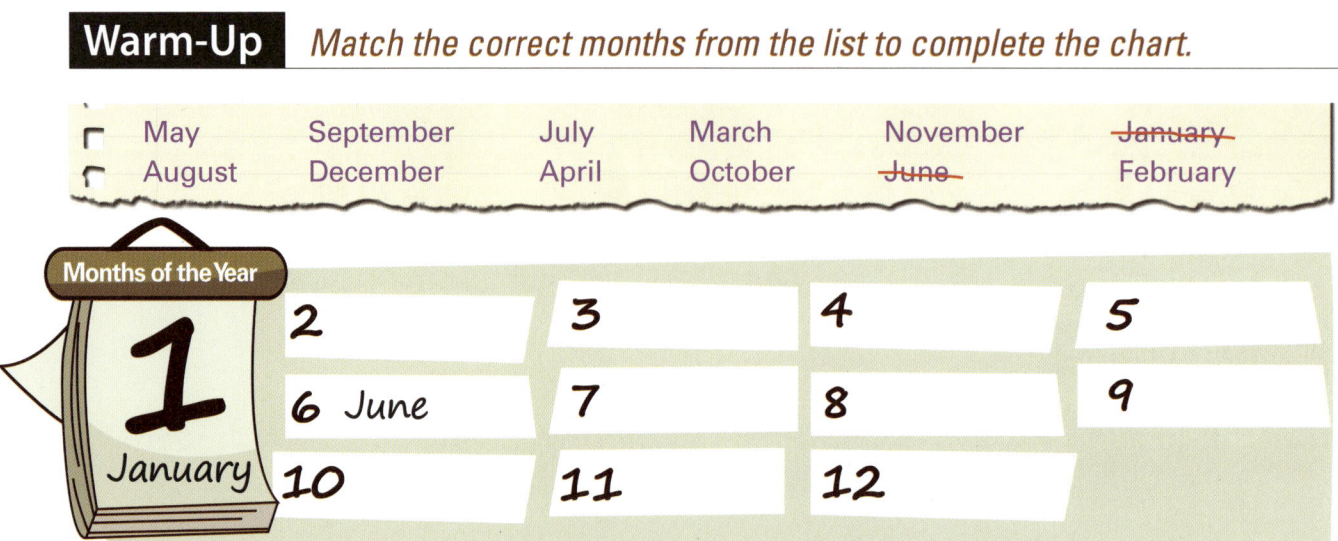

◆ Match the times from the list to complete the boxes.

| seven ten | twelve fifty-five | ten forty-five | three fifteen | one o'clock |
| eleven fifty | two-o-five | four twenty | eight forty | five thirty |

01:00   02:05   03:15   04:20   05:30

07:10   08:40   10:45   11:50   12:55

Dialogue
Listen to the dialogue and practice.

Jay: Hey, Crystal. What is it?
Crystal: Oh, it's my birthday invitation card.
Jay: Really? **When is the party?**
Crystal: **It's (on) September 15th.** Can you come to my birthday party?
Jay: Sure. **What day is it?**
Crystal: **It's (on) Saturday.**
Jay: **What time is it?**
Crystal: **It's (at) 5 o'clock.**
Jay: Good. I'll see you then.

Comprehension Check!

When is Crystal's birthday? | What day is the party? | What time is the party?

Role-Play

Using the above dialogue, roleplay with your partner using your own personal information.

Grammar Point 1 *Impersonal Pronoun 'it'*

Date
What date is **it** today?
It's April 22nd.

Day
What day is **it** today?
It's Thursday.

Time
What time is **it** now?
It's 10:30.

Grammar Point 2 *Wh-Questions*

Wh-Questions	Answers
What date is it today?	**It**'s May 18th.
What date is the meeting?	**It**'s (on) February 26th.
What day is your anniversary?	**It**'s (on) Friday.
What time is the seminar?	**It**'s (at) 11 o'clock.
When is your graduation?	**It**'s (on) Saturday.

Practice

Practice the dialogue with a partner. See the example below.

birthday party
12.11 / Thurs. / 7:30 p.m.

Example

A: When is your **birthday party**?
B: It's (on) **December 11th**.
A: What day is it?
B: It's (on) **Thursday**.
A: What time is **the party**?
B: It's (at) **7:30 p.m**.

1. graduation day
2.23 / Tues. / 10:30 a.m.

2. Halloween party
10.31 / Fri. / 9:00 p.m.

3. job interview
8.24 / Wed. / 5:00 p.m.

4. farewell party
7.3 / Sat. / 6:00 p.m.

soccer match
1.31 / Sun. / 4:30 p.m.

meeting
9.12 / Thurs. / 11:30 p.m.

wedding
4.16 / Fri. / 7:00 p.m.

seminar
6.21 / Mon. / 2:30 p.m.

concert
5.11 / Sat. / 3:00 p.m.

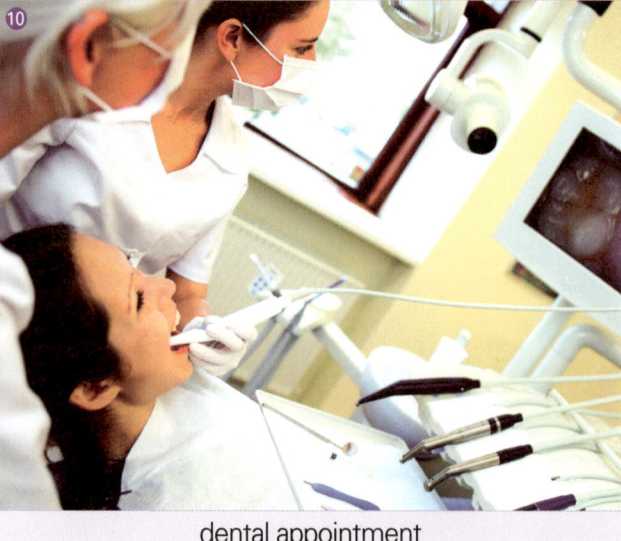

dental appointment
12.3 / Wed. / 5:30 p.m.

Pair Work

   STUDENT A

Divide the class into pairs. One student will be **Student A**, and the other will be **Student B**. Referring to the sample dialogue below, form questions and answers using the information provided.

- : Hi, I'm a big fan of *Jessica*. Are you *Jessica*'s manager?
- : Yes, I am. How may I help you?
- : I want to know *her* schedule. When is the *concert*?
- : It's (on) *July 4th*.
- : What day is it?
- : It's (on) *Friday*.
- : What time is it?
- : It's (at) *4 o'clock*.

1 Ask **Student B** questions about Amy's schedule and complete her schedule book.

Amy's Schedule

Things to do...

- fashion show
- interview
- fan meeting
- wedding

2 Answer **Student B**'s questions based on the information of Paul's schedule.

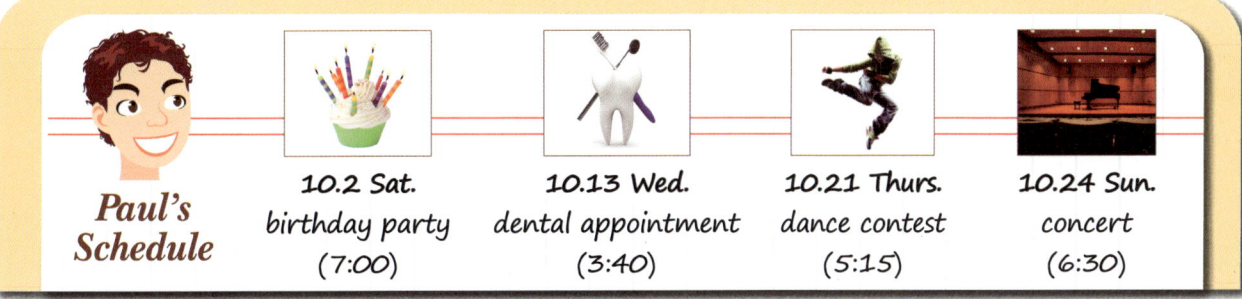

Paul's Schedule

10.2 Sat. birthday party (7:00)

10.13 Wed. dental appointment (3:40)

10.21 Thurs. dance contest (5:15)

10.24 Sun. concert (6:30)

Lesson 8 · 57

Pair Work

STUDENT B

Divide the class into pairs. One student will be **Student A,** and the other will be **Student B.** Referring to the sample dialogue below, form questions and answers using the information provided.

☺ : Hi, I'm a big fan of <u>Jessica</u>. Are you <u>Jessica</u>'s manager?
☺ : Yes, I am. How may I help you?
☺ : I want to know <u>her</u> schedule. When is the <u>concert</u>?
☺ : It's (on) <u>July 4th</u>.
☺ : What day is it?
☺ : It's (on) <u>Friday</u>.
☺ : What time is it?
☺ : It's (at) <u>4 o'clock</u>.

1 Answer *Student A*'s questions based on the information of Amy's schedule.

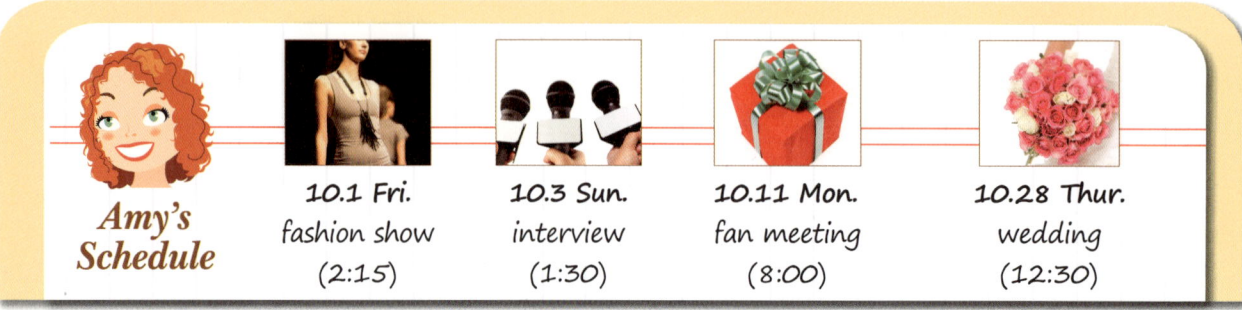

Amy's Schedule

- 10.1 Fri. fashion show (2:15)
- 10.3 Sun. interview (1:30)
- 10.11 Mon. fan meeting (8:00)
- 10.28 Thur. wedding (12:30)

2 Ask *Student A* questions about Paul's schedule and complete his schedule book.

Paul's Schedule

Things to do...
- birthday party
- dental appointment
- dance contest
- concert

Pronunciation — *Listen to the following sentences and repeat after them.*

1 What date is it?
What day is it?

2 It's Tuesday.
It's Thursday.

3 It's June 3rd.
It's June 13th.
It's June 30th.

4 It's February 8th.
It's February 18th.

5 It's 12:15 p.m.
It's 12:50 a.m.

Stretch Out!

Various Ways of Telling Time

▸ **What time is it now? = Do you have the time?**

02:10	It's ten past two.
02:15	It's a quarter past two.
02:30	It's half past two.
02:45	It's a quarter to three.
02:50	It's ten to three.

Lesson 9
I get up at 7 every morning.

Warm-Up Fill in the correct letter from the list below and match it with the correct activity of the daily schedule.

- Word List -

a. brush my teeth	b. watch television	c. have breakfast
d. finish work	e. get up	f. work out at the gym
g. go to work	h. take a shower	i. read a book
j. get dressed	k. have lunch	l. have dinner
m. study English	n. go to bed	o. play computer games

Dialogue — Listen to the dialogue and practice.

Ellen: You are late again.
David: I know. I'm sorry.
   Traffic was heavy this morning.
Ellen: *What time do you get up?*
David: *I get up at 7 every morning.*
   And, *I leave home at 8:10.*
Ellen: *Do you take a bus to work everyday?*
David: *Yes, I do.*
Ellen: The subway is better in the morning.
   I take the subway so I can avoid traffic.

Comprehension Check!
Does David get up at 8 o'clock?
What time does David leave home?
Does David take the subway to work?
Does Ellen take a bus to work?

Role-Play
Using the above dialogue, roleplay with your partner using your own personal information.

Grammar Point 1 *Simple Present : Affirmative / Negative Statements*

Affirmative Statements	Negative Statements
I / You **get up** at 6:15.	I / You **do not get up** at 6:15. (= I / You **don't get up** at 6:15.)
He / She **takes** a shower at 7:20. Peter / Jane **takes** a shower at 7:20.	He / She **does not take** a shower at 7:20. (= He / She **doesn't take** a shower at 7:20.)
We / You / They **go** to school at 8:00.	We / You / They **do not go** to school at 8:00. (= We / You / They **don't go** to school at 8:00.)

▶ Remember!

If the subject is singular, the verb changes its form according to the rules below.

Rules	Examples	Pronunciations
regular verbs → -s	read → read**s** clean → clean**s** get → get**s** take → take**s**	[z] [s]★
-s, -ch, -sh, -z, -x → -es	wash → wash**es** watch → watch**es**	[iz]
consonant + -y → -ies	study → stud**ies**	[z]
vowel + -y → -s	play → play**s**	[z]
irregular verbs	go → **goes** do → **does** have → **has**	[z]

★ only when the sound of the verb ends with [k], [t], [p], [f], [θ]

Grammar Point 2   Simple Present: Yes/No Questions, Wh-Questions

Yes/No Questions	Wh-Questions
Do you get up at 6:15? Yes, I **do**. No, I **don't**.	What time **do you get up**? I **get up** at 6:15.
Does he take a shower at 7:20? Yes, he **does**. No, he **doesn't**.	What time **does he take a shower**? He **takes a shower** at 7:20.
Do they go to school at 8:00? Yes, they **do**. No, they **don't**.	What time **do they go to school**? They **go to school** at 8:00.

Practice   Practice the dialogue with a partner. See the example below.

Kelly
get up / 7:30

you
take a shower / 7:15

Example

A: Does <u>Kelly get up</u> at <u>7:30</u>?
B: No, <u>she</u> doesn't.
A: Then what time does <u>she get up</u>?
B: <u>She gets up</u> at <u>7:00</u>.

A: Do <u>you take a shower</u> at <u>7:15</u>?
B: No, <u>I</u> don't.
A: Then what time do <u>you take a shower</u>?
B: <u>I take a shower</u> at <u>7:30</u>.

Scott
have lunch / 1:00

Jenny
brush her teeth / 6:30

Tom
work out at the gym / 5:15

they
watch television / 9:00

Peter and Sue
play computer games / 8:30

you
get dressed / 7:45

you
study English / 8:00

Anna
go to bed / 12:00

Pair Work

STUDENT A

Divide the class into pairs. One student will be **Student A,** and the other will be **Student B.** Referring to the sample dialogue below, form questions and answers using the information provided.

> ☺ : I want to know about Mike's daily routine.
> ☺ : OK. Ask me.
> ☺ : Does he brush his teeth at 6:50 a.m.?
>
>
>
> **IF yes**
> ☺ : Yes, he does.
> ☺ : Oh, I see. Thanks.
>
> **IF no**
> ☺ : No, he doesn't.
> ☺ : Then, what does he do at 6:50 a.m.?
> ☺ : He gets dressed at 6:50 a.m.
> ☺ : Oh, I see. Thanks.

1 Ask **Student B** questions about Mike's morning routine and complete his schedule book.

| go to school | study English | work out at the gym | have lunch |
| have breakfast | take a shower | get up | |

Mike's Morning

6:40 A.M.		8:30 A.M.	
7:00 A.M.		9:00 A.M.	
8:00 A.M.		10:15 A.M.	
		12:00 P.M.	

2 Answer **Student B**'s questions based on Mike's evening routine.

Mike's Evening

6:40 P.M.	go home	9:30 P.M.	play computer games
7:30 P.M.	have dinner	10:00 P.M.	watch television
8:30 P.M.	read a book	11:00 P.M.	study English
		12:30 A.M.	go to bed

Pair Work

Divide the class into pairs. One student will be **Student A,** and the other will be **Student B.** Referring to the sample dialogue below, form questions and answers using the information provided.

😊 : I want to know about Mike's daily routine.
😊 : OK. Ask me.
😊 : Does he brush his teeth at 6:50 a.m.?

😊 : Yes, he does.
😊 : Oh, I see. Thanks.

😊 : No, he doesn't.
😊 : Then, what does he do at 6:50 a.m.?
😊 : He gets dressed at 6:50 a.m.
😊 : Oh, I see. Thanks.

1 Answer **Student A**'s questions based on Mike's morning routine.

Mike's Morning

Time	Activity	Time	Activity
6:40 A.M.	get up	8:30 A.M.	have breakfast
7:00 A.M.	work out at the gym	9:00 A.M.	go to school
8:00 A.M.	take a shower	10:15 A.M.	study English
		12:00 P.M.	have lunch

2 Ask **Student A** questions about Mike's evening routine and complete his schedule book.

watch television   go to bed   read a book   go home
have dinner   study English   play computer games

Mike's Evening

Time	Activity	Time	Activity
6:40 P.M.		9:30 P.M.	
7:30 P.M.		10:00 P.M.	
8:30 P.M.		11:00 P.M.	
		12:30 A.M.	

Pronunciation
Listen to the following sentences and repeat after them.

1. He **reads** everyday.
   They **read** everyday.

2. I **watch** TV at 9:00.
   She **watches** TV at 9:00.

3. Jenny usually **gets up** at 7:30.
   Peter and Sam usually **get up** at 7:30.

4. We **have** breakfast every morning.
   She **has** breakfast every morning.

5. **Do** you go to bed at 10:00?
   Does he go to bed at 10:00?

6. What **do** you do at 8:00 in the morning?
   What **does** she do at 8:00 in the morning?

Stretch Out!

Tongue Twisters

- She **sells** seashells by the sea shore. The shells that she **sells** are seashells, she's sure.

- Denise **sees** the fleeces. Denise **sees** the fleas. Denise could sneeze and feed and freeze the fleas.

- Luke's duck **likes** lakes. Luke Luck **licks** lakes. Luke's duck **licks** lakes. Duck **takes** licks in lakes Luke Luck **likes.** Luke Luck **takes** licks in lakes duck **likes.**

Lesson 9 · 67

Lesson 10
What do you do?

Warm-Up — *Match the job titles with the corresponding work places.*

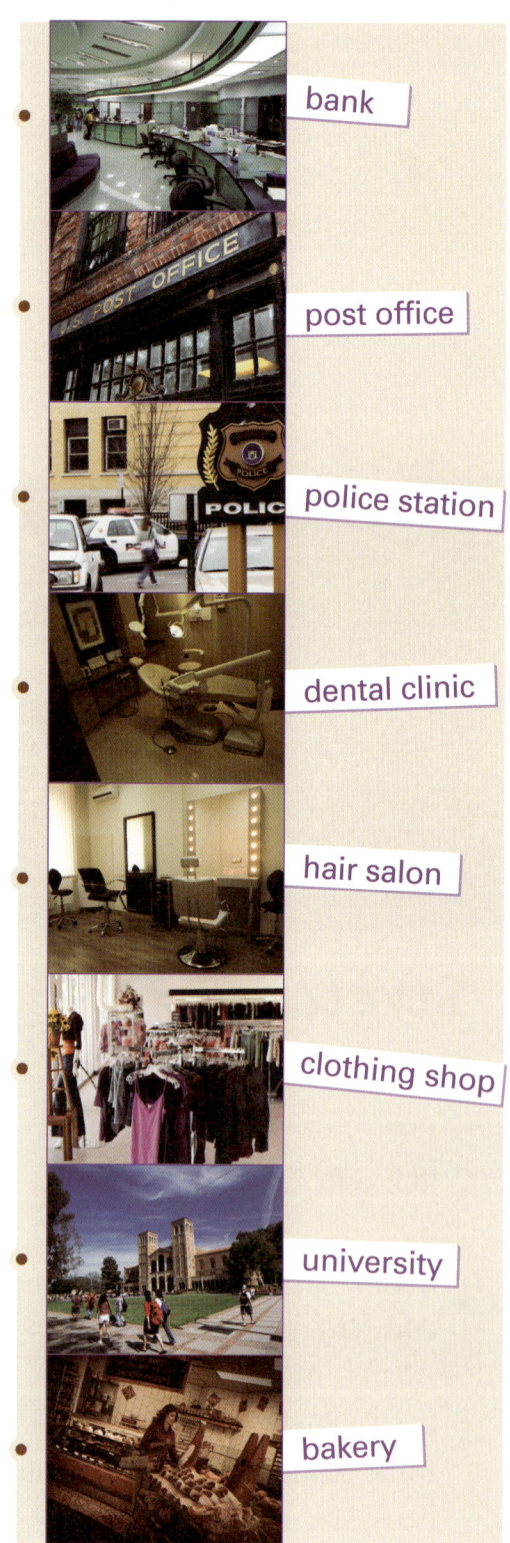

Dialogue — Listen to the dialogue and practice.

Kelly: So, Chris. **What do you do?**
Chris: **I'm a dentist.** What about you?
Kelly: **I'm a banker.**
Chris: Oh, really? **Where do you work?**
Kelly: **I work at an international bank.** What about you?
Chris: **I work at a dental clinic downtown.**
Kelly: Oh, I see.

Comprehension Check!

What is the woman's job? | What is the man's job?
Where does the woman work? | Where does the man work?

Role-Play

Using the above dialogue, roleplay with your partner using your own personal information.

Grammar Point — Simple Present : Wh-Questions

Wh-questions	Affirmative Answers
What do you do?	I**'m** a police officer./We**'re** police officers.
What does he/she do?	He/She**'s** an office worker.
What do they do?	They**'re** clerks.
Where do you work?	I **work** at a police station./We **work** at a police station.
Where does he/she work?	He/She **works** at a post office.
Where do they work?	They **work** at a clothing shop.

Lesson 10 · 69

Practice
Practice the dialogue with a partner. See the example below.

Example

Peter
a clerk / a clothing shop

Jim and Kate
office workers / a post office

A: What does **Peter** do?
B: **He's a clerk**.
A: Where does **he** work?
B: **He** works at **a clothing shop**.

A: What do **Jim and Kate** do?
B: **They're office workers**.
A: Where do **they** work?
B: **They** work at **a post office**.

1
Susan
a banker / a bank

2
Tom
a baker / a bakery

3
Andy and Mary
police officers / a police station

4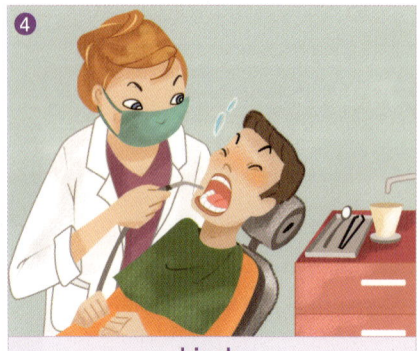
Linda
a dentist / a dental clinic

5
Jack
a professor / a university

6
Brian and Lisa
hairstylists / a hair salon

Pair Work

STUDENT A

Divide the class into pairs. One student will be **Student A,** and the other will be **Student B**. Referring to the sample dialogue below, form questions and answers using the information provided.

😀 : Do you know **Michelle**?
☺ : Yes, **she** is my friend.
😀 : What does **Michelle** do?
☺ : **She** is a **clerk**.
😀 : Where does **she** work?
☺ : **She** works **at a clothing shop**.
😀 : What days does **she** work?
☺ : **She** works **from Tuesday to Saturday**.

Michelle

1 Ask **Student B** for the missing information and complete the table below.

Becky
- _____
- _____
- from Monday to Friday

Amy
- _____
- at a bank
- _____

Tim
- _____
- _____
- Wednesdays and Fridays

2 Answer **Student B**'s questions using the information below.

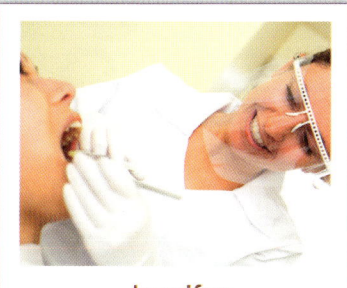

Jennifer
- dentist
- at a dental clinic
- Tuesdays and Fridays

John
- baker
- at a bakery
- from Monday to Saturday

Max
- police officer
- at a police station
- from Monday to Saturday

Pair Work

STUDENT B

Divide the class into pairs. One student will be **Student A,** and the other will be **Student B.** Referring to the sample dialogue below, form questions and answers using the information provided.

☺ : Do you know Michelle?
☺ : Yes, she is my friend.
☺ : What does Michelle do?
☺ : She is a clerk.
☺ : Where does she work?
☺ : She works at a clothing shop.
☺ : What days does she work?
☺ : She works from Tuesday to Saturday.

Michelle

1 Answer Student A's questions using the information below.

Becky
- hairstylist
- at a hair salon
- from Monday to Friday

Amy
- banker
- at a bank
- from Monday to Friday

Tim
- professor
- at a university
- Wednesdays and Fridays

2 Ask Student A for the missing information and complete the table below.

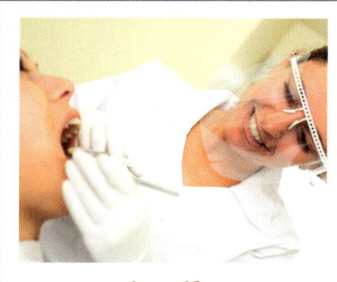
Jennifer
- _____
- _____
- Tuesdays and Fridays

John
- _____
- at a bakery
- _____

Max
- police officer
- _____
- _____

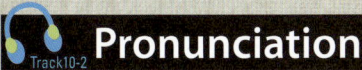

Pronunciation *Listen to the following sentences and repeat after them.*

1. What do you do?
   What do they do?

2. We're bakers.
   We're bankers.

3. She works at a dental clinic.
   He works at a dental clinic.

4. What does he do?
   What does she do?

5. She's an office worker.
   He's an office worker.

6. Where does he work?
   Where do they work?

Stretch Out!

Various Ways to Ask about Someone's Occupation

- What is your job?
- What's your occupation?
- What do you do for a living?
- What business are you in?
- What company do you work for?

Lesson 10 · 73

Lesson 11
I'm doing my homework.

Warm-Up Fill in the blanks with the correct expressions.

– Expressions –

is reading a book	are playing basketball	is doing her homework
is cleaning the room	is checking his e-mail	is sleeping
is listening to music	are working out	are cooking dinner
are watching TV	is singing a song	is playing the piano

Robert _____.
Peter and Amy _____.
Beth _____.
Mary _____.
Tim _____.
Andrew and Chris _____.
Antonio _____.
Steve _____.
Linda and Stacey _____.
Greg are Kathy _____.
Sarah _____.
Pam _____.

Dialogue  Listen to the dialogue and practice.

Mia: Hello, Brad. It's me, Mia. What are you doing?
Brad: Oh, hi Mia. *I'm reading a book.* What about you?
Mia: *I'm doing my homework.* Hey, do you have any plans for tonight?
Brad: No, why?
Mia: I have two free tickets for a movie. Do you want to go to the movies tonight?
Brad: Sure, that sounds like fun!

Comprehension Check!
What is Brad doing? | What is Mia doing?

Role-Play
Using the above dialogue, roleplay with your partner using your own personal information.

Grammar Point 1 — Present Progressive : Affirmative & Negative Statements

Affirmative Statements	Negative Statements
I**'m reading** a book.	I**'m not reading** a book.
You**'re watching** TV.	You**'re not watching** TV. (= **aren't watching**)
He/She/It**'s singing** a song.	He/She/It**'s not singing** a song. (= **isn't singing**)
We**'re cooking** dinner.	We**'re not cooking** dinner. (= **aren't cooking**)
You**'re playing** the piano.	You**'re not playing** the piano. (= **aren't playing**)
They**'re listening** to music.	They**'re not listening** to music. (= **aren't listening**)

Grammar Point 2 Present Progressive: Yes/No Questions

Yes/No Questions	Short Answers	
Am I **cleaning** the room?	Yes, you **are**.	No, you **aren't**.
Are you **playing** basketball?	Yes, I **am**.	No, I**'m not**.
Is he/she/it **sleeping**?	Yes, he/she/it **is**.	No, he/she/it **isn't**.
Are we **working out**?	Yes, you **are**.	No, you **aren't**.
Are you **doing** your homework?	Yes, we **are**.	No, we **aren't**.
Are they **checking** their e-mails?	Yes, they **are**.	No, they **aren't**.

Practice Practice the dialogue with a partner. See the example below.

Alice
✗ play the piano
○ listen to music

Example

A: Is Alice playing the piano?
B: No, she isn't.
    She's listening to music.

1

Kate
✗ do her homework
○ read a book

2

Sarah and Jenna
✗ watch TV
○ cook dinner

3

Tim
✗ listen to music
○ checking his e-mail

4

Nicole
✗ sleep
○ play basketball

5

Sue and Pete
✗ clean the room
○ work out

6

Andy
✗ read a book
○ sing

Pair Work

Divide the class into pairs. One student will be **Student A,** and the other will be **Student B.** Referring to the sample dialogue below, form questions and answers using the information provided.

☺ : Let me guess who Joe is. Is Joe sleeping?
☺ : No, he isn't sleeping.
☺ : Then, is he watching TV?
☺ : No, he isn't watching TV.
☺ : Let me see… Is he reading a book?
☺ : Yes, he is reading a book. That is Joe.

Ask **Student B** questions about the people listed in the left column and fill in the boxes with the corresponding names.

Mark
Nicole
Steve
Susan

Lesson 11 · 77

Pair Work

STUDENT B

Divide the class into pairs. One student will be **Student A,** and the other will be **Student B**. Referring to the sample dialogue below, form questions and answers using the information provided.

☺ : Let me guess who <u>Joe</u> is. Is <u>Joe sleeping</u>?
☺ : No, he <u>isn't sleeping</u>.
☺ : Then, is <u>he watching TV</u>?
☺ : No, <u>he isn't watching TV</u>.
☺ : Let me see… Is <u>he reading a book</u>?
☺ : Yes, <u>he is reading a book</u>. That is <u>Joe</u>.

Ask **Student A** questions about the people listed in the left column and fill in the boxes with the corresponding names.

Christine
Alex
Monica
Richard

Pronunciation
Listen to the following sentences and repeat after them.

1 I am cooking dinner.
I'm cooking dinner.

2 Is she checking her e-mail?
Is he checking his e-mail?

3 We are not doing our homework.
We aren't doing our homework.

4 He's not checking his e-mail.
He isn't checking his e-mail.

5 They're working out.
They aren't working out.

6 We are playing basketball.
We're playing basketball.

Stretch Out!

Additional Expressions about Daily Activities

- study for a test
- go for a walk
- send text messages
- have dinner with friends
- wait for the bus / subway / taxi
- walk the dog
- take a nap
- surf the Internet
- talk to a friend on messenger
- have a meeting

Lesson 12

What are you doing?

Warm-Up *Fill in the boxes with the corresponding names.*

- **Victor** is making the bed.
- **Dorothy** is brushing her teeth.
- **Kelly** is getting dressed.
- **Emma** is setting the table.
- **Susie and Alex** are having a chat.
- **Max** is washing his hands.
- **Paul** is taking a shower.
- **Brian** is making coffee.
- **Rick and Ron** are doing the laundry.
- **Celia** is parking the car.
- **Erin** is putting on makeup.
- **Danny** is doing the dishes.

Dialogue
Listen to the dialogue and practice.

Stacey: Eric, where are you?
Eric: I'm in the kitchen.
Stacey: *What are you doing there?*
Eric: *I'm doing the dishes.* Stacey, can you come over here? Please roll up my sleeves. They're getting wet.
Stacey: Okay, no problem.

Comprehension Check!
Where is Eric? | What is Eric doing?

Role-Play
Using the above dialogue, roleplay with your partner using your own personal information.

Grammar Point — Present Progressive: Wh-Questions (What)

Wh-questions (What)	Short Answers
What am I **doing**?	You**'re making** coffee.
What are you **doing**?	I**'m setting** the table.
What is he/she/it **doing**?	She/He/It**'s taking** a shower.
What are we **doing**?	You**'re doing** the laundry.
What are you **doing**?	We**'re washing** our hands.
What are they **doing**?	They**'re putting** on makeup.

★ Point!

| make → making | take → taking | have → having |
| get → getting | set → setting | put → putting |

Practice
Practice the dialogue with a partner. See the example below.

Stella
wash her hands / brush her teeth

Example

A: Is <u>Stella washing her hands</u>?
B: No, <u>she isn't</u>.
A: Then, what <u>is she</u> doing?
B: <u>She's brushing her teeth</u>.

1 Stacey
get dressed / park the car

2 Greg
do the dishes / do the laundry

3 Lily
put on makeup / make the bed

4 Susan and Stella
set the table / make coffee

5 Michael
take a shower / brush his teeth

6 Joe and Sue
get dressed / have a chat

Pair Work

STUDENT A

Divide the class into pairs. One student will be **Student A,** and the other will be **Student B.** Referring to the sample dialogue below, form questions and answers using the information provided.

☺ : Is Kate home?
☺ : Is she doing the laundry?
☺ : Then, what is she doing?
☺ : Why do you ask?

☺ : Yes, she is.
☺ : No, she isn't.
☺ : She's making the bed.
☺ : I need her help.

Kate / make the bed

1 Ask **Student B** questions about the people listed below and fill in the table with what he or she is actually doing.

	Brad	Susan	Frank	Cindy
Is he/she ~ ing?	get dressed	do the dishes	brush his teeth	park the car
What is he/she doing?				

2 Answer **Student B**'s questions based on the information below.

Ida — set the table

Wendy — park the car

Ellen — brush her teeth

Paul — do the laundry

Pair Work

STUDENT B

Divide the class into pairs. One student will be **Student A**, and the other will be **Student B**. Referring to the sample dialogue below, form questions and answers using the information provided.

- 😊 : Is <u>Kate</u> home?
- 😊 : <u>Is she doing the laundry</u>?
- 😊 : Then, what <u>is she</u> doing?
- 😊 : I need <u>her</u> help.

- 😊 : Yes, <u>she</u> is.
- 😊 : <u>No, she isn't</u>.
- 😊 : <u>She's making the bed</u>. Why do you ask?

Kate / make the bed

1 Answer **Student A**'s questions based on the information below.

Brad — take a shower

Susan — have a chat

Frank — make coffee

Cindy — wash her hands

2 Ask **Student A** questions about the people listed below and fill in the table with what he or she is actually doing.

	Ida	Wendy	Ellen	Paul
Is he/she ~ ing?	make coffee	wash her hands	put on makeup	make the bed
What is he/she doing?				

i Can Speak **1 Red** 84

Pronunciation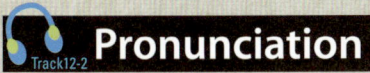

Listen to the following sentences and repeat after them.

1. Is she getting dressed?
   Is he getting dressed?

2. She's doing the laundry.
   She's doing the dishes.

3. What is she doing?
   What is he doing?

4. Is he making the bed?
   Is he making coffee?

5. They are putting on makeup.
   They're putting on makeup.

6. We're brushing our teeth.
   You're brushing your teeth.

Stretch Out!

Additional Expressions about Things You Do at Home

- get up
- vacuum the room
- hang the laundry
- mow the lawn
- watch TV news / soap opera

- go to bed
- clean the house
- shampoo / dry one's hair
- wash the car
- make breakfast / lunch / dinner

Lesson 13

I can play tennis.

Warm-Up *Match the activities to the corresponding pictures.*

– Expressions –

play the drums	ride a bicycle	swim	play soccer
play the guitar	paint	snowboard	play golf
play the flute	drive a car	bowl	play baseball
play the violin	cook	ski	play tennis

Dialogue
Listen to the dialogue and practice.

Ron: So, Alice. **Can you ride a bicycle?**
Alice: **No, I can't. I can't ride a bicycle.**
Ron: Then, what about sports? **Can you play golf?**
Alice: **No, I can't. But I can play tennis.**
Ron: **I can play tennis, too.** Do you want to play tennis on Saturday?
Alice: That sounds great!

Comprehension Check!
Can Alice ride a bicycle? | Can Alice play golf? | Can Alice play tennis?

Role-Play
Using the above dialogue, roleplay with your partner using your own personal information.

Grammar Point   *Can (ability)*

Affirmative Statements	Negative Statements
I **can** drive.	I **can't** drive.
You **can** play the violin.	You **can't** play the violin.
He/She/It **can** swim.	He/She/It **can't** swim.
We **can** play tennis.	We **can't** play tennis.
You **can** cook.	You **can't** cook.
They **can** snowboard.	They **can't** snowboard.

Questions	Short Answers	
Can I paint?	Yes, you **can**.	No, you **can't**.
Can you play golf?	Yes, I **can**.	No, I **can't**.
Can he/she/it swim?	Yes, he/she/it **can**.	No, he/she/it **can't**.
Can we play the drums?	Yes, you **can**.	No, you **can't**.
Can you bowl?	Yes, we **can**.	No, we **can't**.
Can they ski?	Yes, they **can**.	No, they **can't**.

Practice
Practice the dialogue with a partner. See the example below.

Example

A: Can Amanda play the guitar?
B: Yes, she can, but she can't play the drums.

Pair Work

STUDENT A

Divide the class into pairs. One student will be **Student A**, and the other will be **Student B**. Referring to the sample dialogue below, form questions and answers using the information provided.

☺ : Let's do something on the weekend.
☺ : Sounds like fun.
☺ : What can we do together? Can you **play baseball**?

☺ : Yes, I can.

☺ : No, I can't **play baseball**.
☺ : Then, can you **ski**? (continue)

First, check (✓) what you **can** or **can't** do. Then, ask each other questions and find out what your partner **can** or **can't** do.

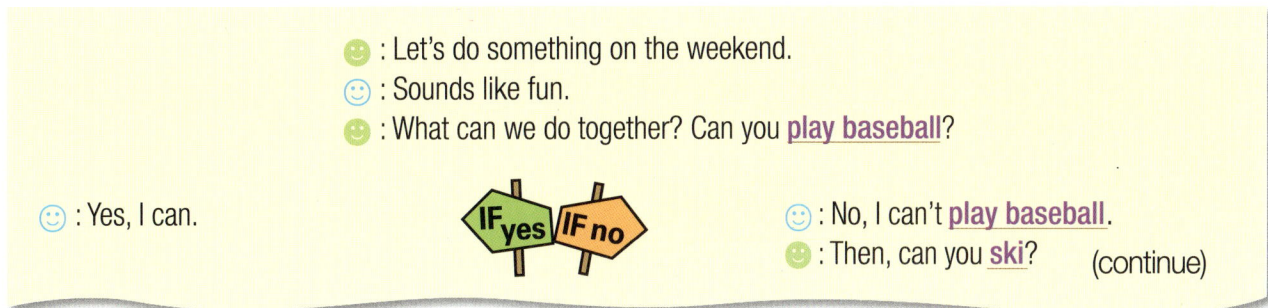

Pair Work

STUDENT B

Divide the class into pairs. One student will be **Student A**, and the other will be **Student B**. Referring to the sample dialogue below, form questions and answers using the information provided.

☺ : Let's do something on the weekend.
☺ : Sounds like fun.
☺ : What can we do together? Can you <u>play baseball</u>?

☺ : Yes, I can.

☺ : No, I can't <u>play baseball</u>.
☺ : Then, can you <u>ski</u>? (continue)

First, check (✓) what you *can* or *can't* do. Then, ask each other questions and find out what your partner *can* or *can't* do.

Pronunciation
Listen to the following sentences and repeat after them.

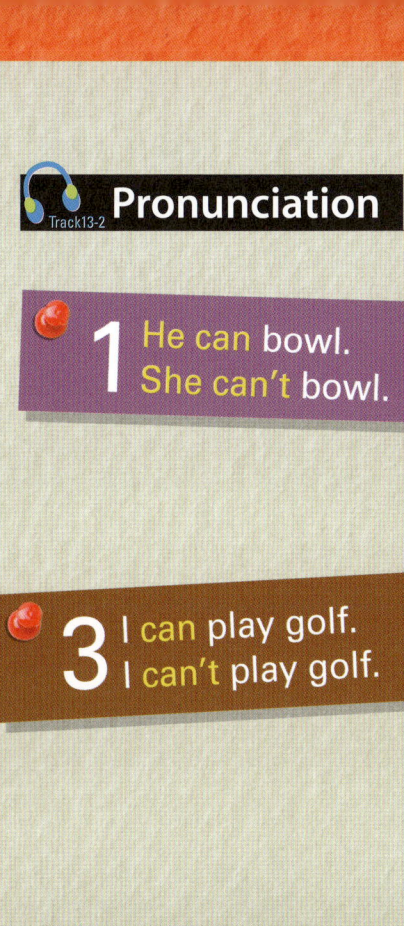

1. He can bowl.
   She can't bowl.

2. Can they play the drums?
   Can you play the drums?

3. I can play golf.
   I can't play golf.

4. We can snowboard.
   They can't snowboard.

5. Can he play the violin?
   Can she play the violin?

6. She can ride a bicycle.
   He can't ride a bicycle.

Stretch Out!

Various Ways to Ask about Abilities

Q	A
Can you play football well?	Yes, I'm a good football player.
Are you good at playing table tennis?	Well, only a little, but I'm good at playing pool.
Are you a good hockey player?	No, I can't play hockey at all.
What are you good at?	I'm good at dancing.
What sports can you play?	I can play volleyball.
What musical instruments can you play?	I can play the cello.

Lesson 14
Could you turn off the TV?

Warm-Up Complete the questions with the corresponding expressions.

– Expressions –

water the plants	pass me the salt	close the window
pick up the mail	open the door	turn on the light
take out the garbage	turn down the volume	turn off the TV

Dialogue Listen to the dialogue and practice.

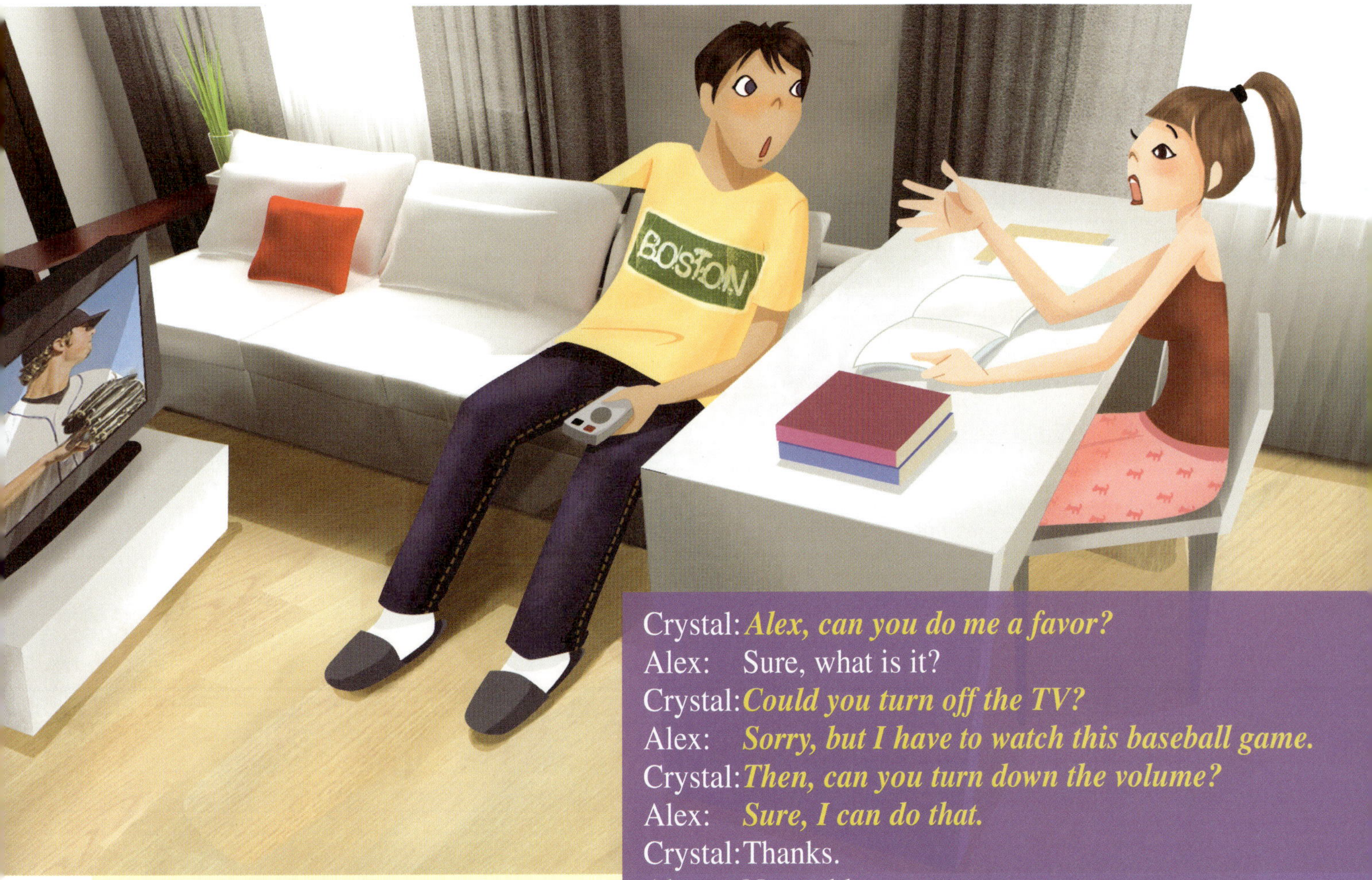

Crystal: *Alex, can you do me a favor?*
Alex: Sure, what is it?
Crystal: *Could you turn off the TV?*
Alex: *Sorry, but I have to watch this baseball game.*
Crystal: *Then, can you turn down the volume?*
Alex: *Sure, I can do that.*
Crystal: Thanks.
Alex: No problem.

Comprehension Check!
Can Alex turn off the TV? | Can Alex turn down the volume?

Role-Play
Using the above dialogue, roleplay with your partner using your own personal information.

Grammar Point   Can, Could (request)

Making Requests	
Formal	**Informal**
Could you open the door?	**Can you** close the window?

Accepting	Refusing
Sure, I can.	No, I can't.
Of course.	I'm afraid I can't.
Certainly.	I'm sorry, but I'm very busy.
No problem.	Sorry, but I'm on the phone right now.

Lesson 14 · 93

Practice

Practice the dialogue with a partner. See the example below.

Example

○ open the door
Okay, no problem.

A: Could you **open the door**?
B: **Okay, no problem**.
A: Thanks a lot.

✕ close the window
I want to get some fresh air.

A: Can **you close the window**?
B: Sorry, but can you wait a moment?
I want to get some fresh air.
A: Oh, I see. It's okay, then.

1

○ turn down the volume
Sure, I can.

2

○ water the plants
Okay, no problem.

3

✕ take out the garbage
I'm on the phone right now.

4

○ turn off the light
Certainly.

5

○ pass me the salt
Of course.

6

✕ pick up the mail
I'm busy now.

i Can Speak **1 Red** 94

Pair Work

STUDENT A

Divide the class into pairs. One student will be **Student A**, and the other will be **Student B**. Referring to the sample dialogue below, form questions and answers using the information provided.

☺ : Could you do me a favor?
☺ : Sure, what is it?
☺ : Could you <u>open the window</u> for me?

☺ : Sure, I can. / No problem. / Of course. / Certainly.
☺ : Thanks a lot. I really appreciate it.

☺ : I'm sorry, but <u>it's too cold</u>.
☺ : Oh, it's okay. Don't worry about it.

1 Ask **Student B** questions to make requests for the following things and check (✓) the appropriate box in the table based on your partner's answers.

My requests

	turn down the volume	turn off the light	take out the garbage	close the window
Accept	☐	☐	☐	☐
Refuse (reasons)	☐	☐	☐	☐

2 Answer **Student B**'s questions using the information in the table below. When you refuse a request, tell him/her the reason.

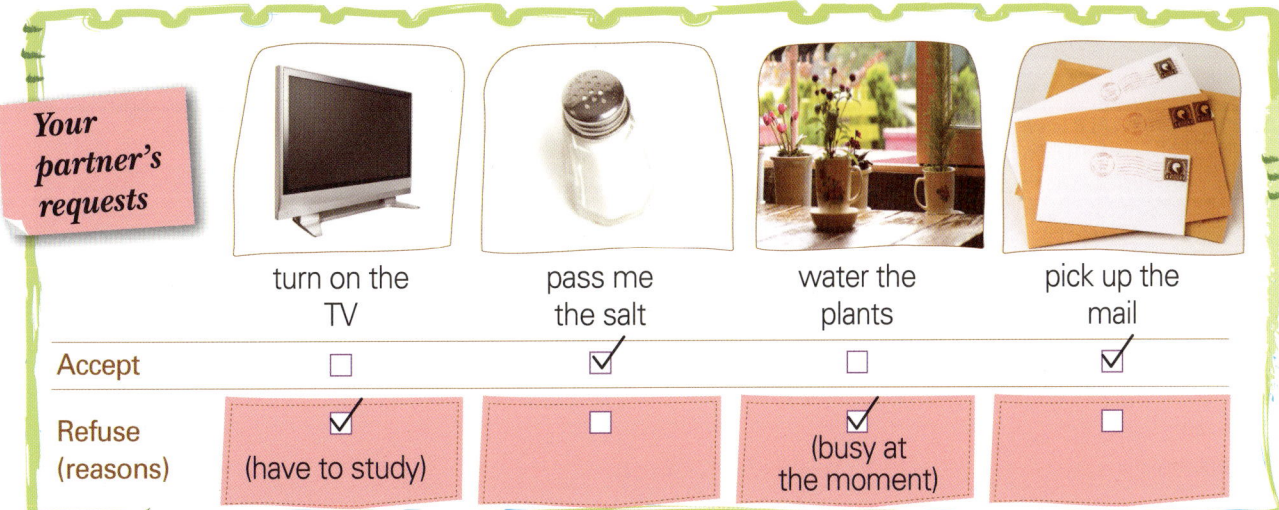

Your partner's requests

	turn on the TV	pass me the salt	water the plants	pick up the mail
Accept	☐	✓	☐	✓
Refuse (reasons)	✓ (have to study)	☐	✓ (busy at the moment)	☐

Pair Work

STUDENT B

Divide the class into pairs. One student will be *Student A*, and the other will be *Student B*. Referring to the sample dialogue below, form questions and answers using the information provided.

☺ : Could you do me a favor?
☺ : Sure, what is it?
☺ : Could you <u>open the window</u> for me?

☺ : Sure, I can. / No problem. / Of course. / Certainly.
☺ : Thanks a lot. I really appreciate it.

☺ : I'm sorry, but <u>it's too cold</u>.
☺ : Oh, it's okay. Don't worry about it.

1 Answer *Student A*'s questions using the information in the table below. When you refuse a request, tell him/her the reason.

Your partner's requests

	turn down the volume	turn off the light	take out the garbage	close the window
Accept	✓	✓	☐	☐
Refuse (reasons)	☐	☐	✓ (do the laundry)	✓ (too hot)

2 Ask *Student A* questions to make requests for the following things and check (✓) the appropriate box in the table based on your partner's answers.

My requests

	turn on the TV	pass me the salt	water the plants	pick up the mail
Accept	☐	☐	☐	☐
Refuse (reasons)	☐	☐	☐	☐

Pronunciation
Listen to the following sentences and repeat after them.

1. Can you pick up the mail?
   Could you pick up the mail?

2. Sorry, but I'm on the phone right now.
   Sorry, but I'm doing the laundry right now.

3. Could you turn off the light?
   Could you turn on the light?

4. I'm afraid I can't open the window.
   I'm afraid I can't close the window.

5. Can you turn on the TV?
   Can you turn off the TV?

6. Could you pass me the salt?
   Can you pass me the salt?

Stretch Out!

Additional Expressions about Making Requests

Formal	Informal
Could you shut the door?	Can you carry this box?
Would you turn on the air conditioner?	Will you answer the phone?
Could you give me a ride?	Can you clean up the room?
Would you turn off the heater?	Will you be quiet?

Lesson 15

Is there any milk?

Warm-Up *Fill in the boxes with the corresponding words.*

– Word List –

mushrooms	grapes	~~flour~~	eggs	coffee	oranges
cucumbers	soda	tomatoes	~~juice~~	cakes	potatoes
cheese	~~milk~~	ice cream	cookies		

Dialogue  Listen to the dialogue and practice.

Tyler: Hey, Liz. Let's go to the grocery store.
Liz: Okay. Let me check the fridge.
Tyler: *Is there any milk?*
Liz: *No, there isn't any milk left.*
Tyler: What about eggs? *Are there any eggs?*
Liz: *Yes, there are many left.*
Tyler: Then, let's go buy some milk.

Comprehension Check!
Is there any milk in the fridge? | Are there any eggs in the fridge?

Role-Play
Using the above dialogue, roleplay with your partner using your own personal information.

Grammar Point — Countable and Uncountable Nouns

	Singular	Plural
Countable Noun	**an** orange	two orange**s**
Uncountable Noun	milk	X

Countable Nouns	Uncountable Nouns
some / any	some / any
many / a lot of	**much** / a lot of
a few	**a little**

Lesson 15 · 99

Practice
Practice the dialogue with a partner. See the example below.

Example

A: I need some **grapes**. **Are** there any **grapes** on the table?
B: Let me check. Oh, there **are** some **grapes**. Here you are.
A: Thanks a lot.

A: I need some **milk**. **Is** there any **milk** on the table?
B: Let me check. I'm sorry, there **isn't** any **milk**.
A: It's okay.

❶  juice	❷  tomatoes	❸  mushrooms
❹  cheese	❺  eggs	❻  oranges

Pair Work

STUDENT A

Divide the class into pairs. One student will be **Student A**, and the other will be **Student B**. Referring to the sample dialogue below, form questions and answers using the information provided.

☺ : I'm going to the grocery store. <u>Is there any juice</u> in the refrigerator?
☺ : Yes, there is <u>a little juice</u> in the fridge.
☺ : Shall we get some more from the grocery store?
☺ : <u>Yes, we need some more</u>.

☺ : I'm going to the grocery store. <u>Are there any eggs</u> in the refrigerator?
☺ : Yes, there are <u>many eggs</u> in the fridge.
☺ : Shall we get some more from the grocery store?
☺ : <u>No, we don't have to</u>.

1 Ask **Student B** questions about the following things and fill in the table based on your partner's answers.

	potatoes	cheese	soda	mushrooms
How much / many?				
Need	☐	☐	☐	☐
Don't need	☐	☐	☐	☐

2 Answer **Student B**'s questions based on the information in the table below.

	milk	tomatoes	grapes	ice cream
How much / many?	much	a few	some	a little
Need	☐	✓	☐	✓
Don't need	✓	☐	✓	☐

Lesson 15 · 101

Pair Work

STUDENT B

Divide the class into pairs. One student will be **Student A**, and the other will be **Student B**. Referring to the sample dialogue below, form questions and answers using the information provided.

- 😀 : I'm going to the grocery store. **Is there any juice** in the refrigerator?
- 🙂 : Yes, there is **a little juice** in the fridge.
- 😀 : Shall we get some more from the grocery store?
- 🙂 : **Yes, we need some more**.

- 😀 : I'm going to the grocery store. **Are there any eggs** in the refrigerator?
- 🙂 : Yes, there are **many eggs** in the fridge.
- 😀 : Shall we get some more from the grocery store?
- 🙂 : **No, we don't have to**.

1 Answer **Student A**'s questions based on the information in the table below.

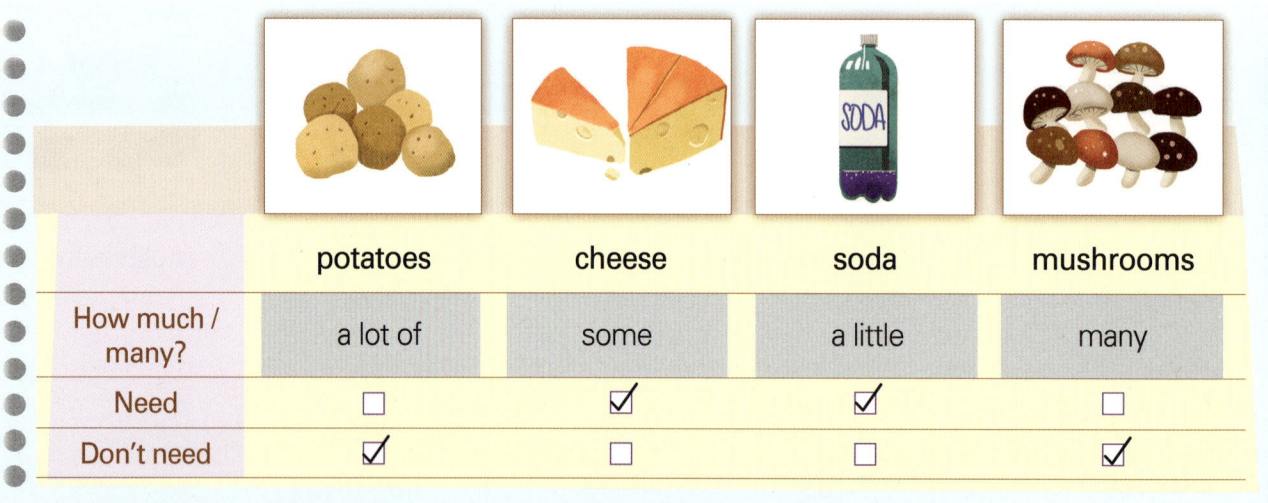

	potatoes	cheese	soda	mushrooms
How much / many?	a lot of	some	a little	many
Need	☐	✓	✓	☐
Don't need	✓	☐	☐	✓

2 Ask **Student A** questions about the following things and fill in the table based on your partner's answers.

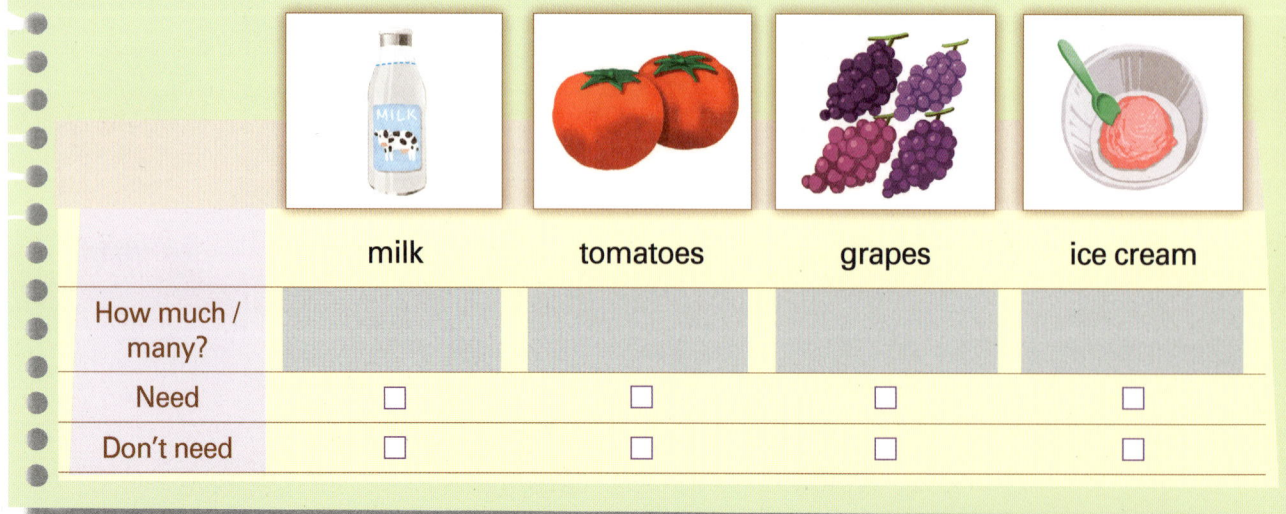

	milk	tomatoes	grapes	ice cream
How much / many?				
Need	☐	☐	☐	☐
Don't need	☐	☐	☐	☐

Pronunciation Listen to the following sentences and repeat after them.

1. There **is** a lot of flour.
   There **isn't** a lot of flour.

2. There **is a potato** in the fridge.
   There **are potatoes** in the fridge.

3. **Is there any** cheese left?
   Are there any grapes left?

4. There **is some** soda.
   There **isn't much** soda.

5. There **are some** oranges in the refrigerator.
   There **aren't any** oranges in the refrigerator.

6. **Is there any** coffee?
   Are there any eggs?

Stretch Out!

Nouns that can be Countable & Uncountable

Countable Nouns	Uncountable Nouns
 a potato  a paper	 potato  paper
 a glass 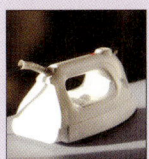 an iron	 glass  iron

Lesson 15 · 103

Lesson 16
I was tired this morning.

Warm-Up *Fill in the blanks with the corresponding words.*

– Word List –

happy	tired	angry	confused	sleepy
nervous	sick	thirsty	sad	scared
surprised	bored	cold	hungry	hot

Dialogue  Listen to the dialogue and practice.

David: Hey, Jenna. I saw you this morning and you didn't look alright. **Were you sick this morning?**
Jenna: **No, I wasn't. I was just tired.** I didn't get much sleep last night.
David: Oh, that's terrible.
Jenna: Don't worry. I'm okay now.
David: That's good to hear.

Comprehension Check!
Was Jenna sick this morning? | Was Jenna tired this morning?

Role-Play
Using the above dialogue, roleplay with your partner using your own personal information.

Grammar Point 1 — Simple Past of Be verb: Affirmative & Negative Statements

Affirmative Statements	Negative Statements
I **was** happy.	I **was not** happy. (= **wasn't**)
You **were** sleepy.	You **were not** sleepy. (= **weren't**)
He/She/It **was** thirsty.	He/She/It **was not** thirsty. (= **wasn't**)
We **were** scared.	We **were not** scared. (= **weren't**)
You **were** surprised.	You **were not** surprised. (= **weren't**)
They **were** confused.	They **were not** confused. (= **weren't**)

Lesson 16 · 105

Grammar Point 2 — Simple Past of Be verb: Yes/No Questions

Yes/No Questions	Short Answers	
Was I nervous?	Yes, you **were**.	No, you **weren't**.
Were you hungry?	Yes, I **was**.	No, I **wasn't**.
Was he/she/it sick?	Yes, he/she/it **was**.	No, he/she/it **wasn't**.
Were we angry?	Yes, you **were**.	No, you **weren't**.
Were you tired?	Yes, we **were**.	No, we **weren't**.
Were they bored?	Yes, they **were**.	No, they **weren't**.

Practice
Practice the dialogue with a partner. See the example below.

Becky
angry / confused

> **Example**
> *A:* **Was Becky angry** this morning?
> *B:* No, **she wasn't angry**.
> **She was** just **confused**.

1 Stella
sick / thirsty

2 Carl
nervous / cold

3 Harold and Nancy
bored / sleepy

4 Julia
tired / hungry

5 Peter
sad / hot

6 Sam and Becky
scared / surprised

Pair Work

STUDENT A

Divide the class into pairs. One student will be **Student A**, and the other will be **Student B**. Referring to the sample dialogue below, form questions and answers using the information provided.

☺ : Let me guess who **Maria** is.
   Was **she sleepy** at the picnic?
☺ : **No, she wasn't**.
☺ : Was **she nervous**?
☺ : **No, she wasn't**.
☺ : Was **she sad**?
☺ : **Yes, she was**.
☺ : Then, **she** must be **Maria**.
☺ : Yes, **she** is.

Ask **Student B** questions about the people listed in the left column and fill in the boxes with the corresponding names.

Kate
Jason
Erica
Paul

Lesson 16 · 107

Pair Work

STUDENT B

Divide the class into pairs. One student will be **Student A**, and the other will be **Student B**. Referring to the sample dialogue below, form questions and answers using the information provided.

☺ : Let me guess who <u>Maria</u> is.
　　Was <u>she sleepy</u> at the picnic?
☺ : Was <u>she nervous</u>?
☺ : Was <u>she sad</u>?
☺ : Then, <u>she</u> must be <u>Maria</u>.

☺ : <u>No, she wasn't</u>.
☺ : <u>No, she wasn't</u>.
☺ : <u>Yes, she was</u>.
☺ : Yes, <u>she</u> is.

Ask **Student A** questions about the people listed in the left column and fill in the boxes with the corresponding names.

Julia
Matthew
Jeff
Amy

Pronunciation
Listen to the following sentences and repeat after them.

1. You **were** nervous.
   You **weren't** nervous.

2. Was **she** annoyed?
   Was **he** annoyed?

3. I **wasn't** sleepy this morning.
   I **was** sleepy this morning.

4. **She** wasn't surprised.
   He wasn't surprised.

5. **Were they** thirsty?
   Was he thirsty?

6. We **weren't** scared.
   We **were** scared.

Stretch Out!

Extra Words Related to Emotions

Positive	Negative
excited	annoyed
delighted	worried
relieved	depressed
pleased	disappointed
satisfied	embarrassed

Lesson 17

Where were you this morning?

Warm-Up *Complete the sentences with the corresponding phrases.*

– Word List –

at the gym	at the office	at the airport	at the bookstore
at the bar	at the movies	at the hospital	at the restaurant
at the park	at the library	at the mall	at the supermarket

I was ____. We were ____. John was ____. You were ____.

They were ____. Janet was ____. Antonio was ____. You were ____.

My boyfriend and I were ____. He was ____. Erica and her roommate were ____. James and Amy were ____.

Dialogue  Listen to the dialogue and practice.

Scott: **Cindy, where were you this morning?** I called you but you weren't home.
Cindy: **Oh, I was at the mall with a friend.**
Scott: **Who were you with?**
Cindy: **I was with Jessica.** Why did you call me?
Scott: I was just bored.

Comprehension Check!
Where was Cindy this morning? | Who was Cindy with?

Role-Play
Using the above dialogue, roleplay with your partner using your own personal information.

Grammar Point — Simple Past of Be verb: Wh-Questions

Wh-Questions	Answers
Where was I last Sunday?	You **were at** the hospital.
Where were you yesterday?	I **was at** the airport.
Where was he/she/it in the morning?	He/She/It **was at** the park.
Where were we on Monday evening?	You **were at** the movies.
Where were you this afternoon?	We **were at** the bookstore.
Where were they at 2 p.m.?	They **were at** the supermarket.
Who was I with?	You **were with** Crystal.
Who were you with?	I **was with** my brother.
Who was he/she/it with?	He/She/It **was with** Helen.
Who were we with?	You **were with** your family.
Who were you with?	We **were with** our sister.
Who were they with?	They **were with** their friends.

Lesson 17 · 111

Practice

Practice the dialogue with a partner. See the example below.

Mary
at the movies / Tom

Example

A: Where was Mary yesterday afternoon?
B: She was at the movies.
A: Who was she with?
B: She was with Tom.

1 Stella
at the supermarket / Eric

2 Diane and Carlos
at the park / their kids

3 Mark
at the bookstore / Sue

4 Jack
at the bar / his girlfriend

5 Erica and Sally
at the gym / Kate

6 Janet
at the library / her classmate

Pair Work

STUDENT A

Divide the class into pairs. One student will be **Student A**, and the other will be **Student B**. Referring to the sample dialogue below, form questions and answers using the information provided.

☺ : Where was **Tim** last night?
  I called **him** at home but nobody picked up.
☺ : **He** was at the **airport**.
☺ : Who was **he** with?
☺ : **He** was with **Jack**.
☺ : What did they do?
☺ : They **picked their brother up**.

☺ : Where were **Kate and Alex** last night?
  I called **them** at home but nobody picked up.
☺ : **They** were at the **library**.
☺ : Who were **they** with?
☺ : **They** were with **their friends**.
☺ : What did they do?
☺ : They **studied for the midterm**.

1 Ask **Student B** questions about what the people in the chart did last night and complete the table below.

	Where?	With who?	What?
Jake			
Alice			
Pam and Andy			
Student B			

2 Answer **Student B**'s questions using the information below. The last box is left for you to talk about what you did the last night.

	Where?	With who?	What?
Lisa	restaurant	John	had dinner
Andrew and Jennie	hospital	Karen	visited their friend
Peter	park	his girlfriend	took a walk
Student A			

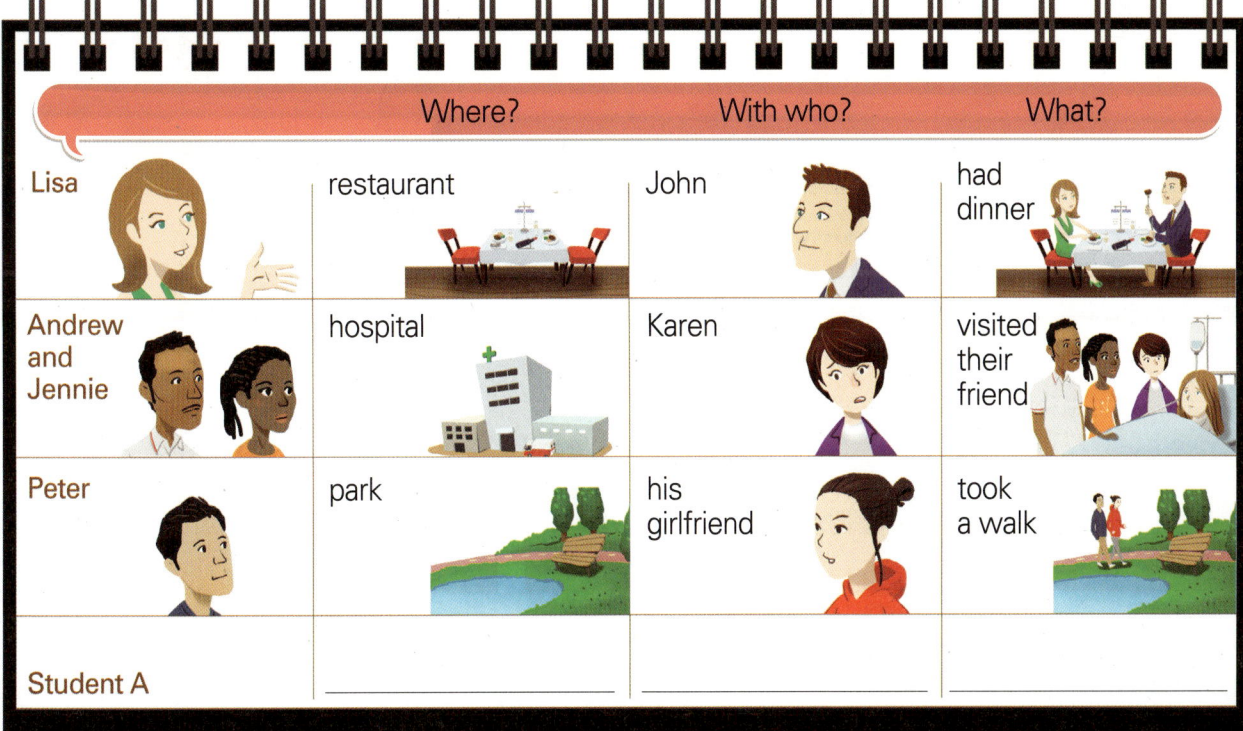

Lesson 17 • 113

Pair Work

STUDENT B

Divide the class into pairs. One student will be **Student A**, and the other will be **Student B**. Referring to the sample dialogue below, form questions and answers using the information provided.

- ☺ : Where was **Tim** last night?
  I called **him** at home but nobody picked up.
- ☺ : **He** was at the **airport**.
- ☺ : Who was **he** with?
- ☺ : **He** was with **Jack**.
- ☺ : What did they do?
- ☺ : They **picked their brother up**.

- ☺ : Where were **Kate and Alex** last night?
  I called **them** at home but nobody picked up.
- ☺ : **They** were at the **library**.
- ☺ : Who were **they** with?
- ☺ : **They** were with **their friends**.
- ☺ : What did they do?
- ☺ : They **studied for the midterm**.

1 Answer **Student A**'s questions using the information below. The last box is left for you to talk about what you did last night.

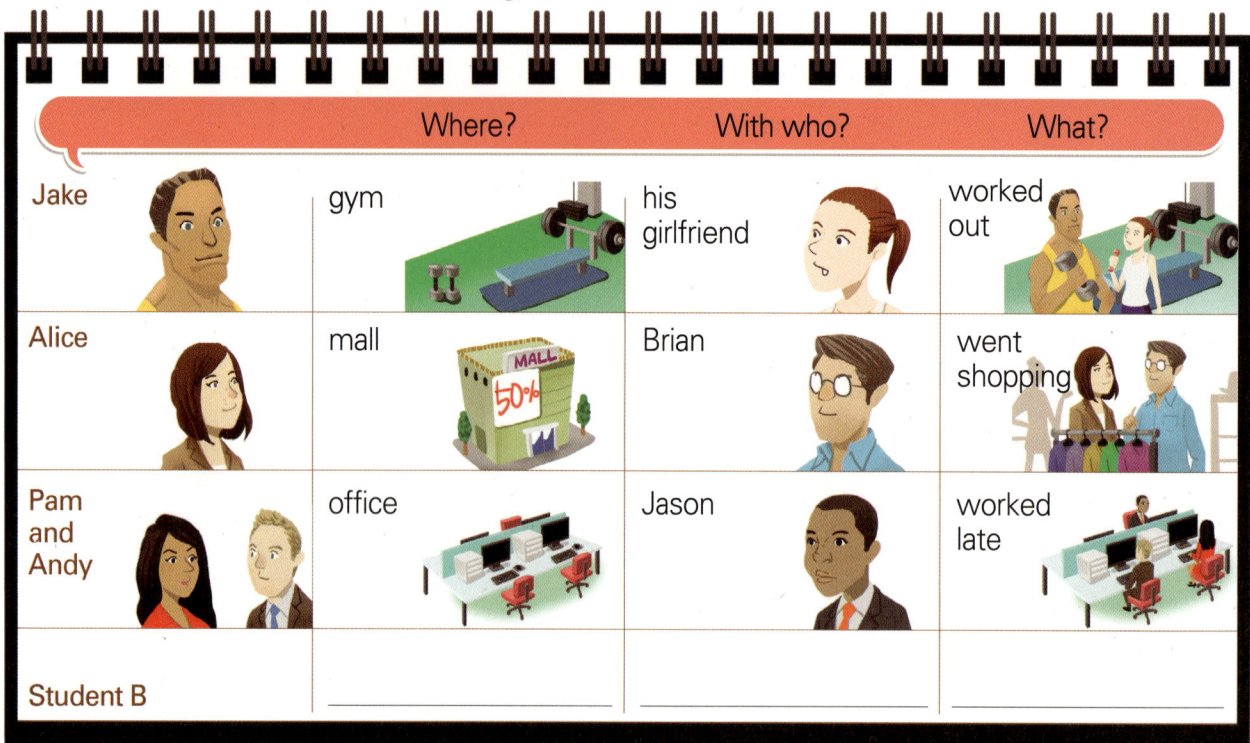

2 Ask **Student A** questions about what the people in the chart did last night and complete the table below.

	Where?	With who?	What?
Lisa			
Andrew and Jennie			
Peter			
Student A			

i Can Speak **1 Red** 114

Pronunciation Listen to the following sentences and repeat after them.

1. Who was he with on Sunday?
   Who was she with on Sunday?

2. Where was she this morning?
   Where was he this morning?

3. I was at the airport yesterday.
   We were at the airport yesterday.

4. Who were you with last night?
   Who were they with last night?

5. He was at the movies with his girlfriend.
   She was at the movies with her boyfriend.

6. We were with our friends.
   You were with your friends.

Stretch Out!

Extra Words Related to Places

- at home
- at work
- at school
- at the museum
- at the bakery
- at the gas station

- at the hotel
- at the bank
- at the cafeteria
- at the theater
- at the drugstore
- at the convenience store

Lesson 17 · 115

Lesson 18
What were you doing at 10 o'clock last night?

Warm-Up Fill in the blanks with the corresponding expressions.

– Expressions –

having a drink	chatting online	meeting her boyfriend
watching a movie	making a phone call	taking a nap
taking a walk	watching a soap opera	walking her dog
grocery shopping	attending a party	going out on a date

She was _____.

You were _____.

They were _____.

Kathy was _____.

Robert was _____.

The dog was _____.

Jessica was _____.

I was _____.

They were _____.

We were _____.

He was _____.

You were _____.

Dialogue — Listen to the dialogue and practice.

Ken: I think I saw you yesterday. *What were you doing at 10 o'clock last night?*
Nicole: *I was having a drink with my co-workers.*
Ken: Where were you?
Nicole: I was at Barney's.
Ken: *I was also having a drink with my friends there.*
Nicole: Oh, wow! Then, we were at the same bar.
Ken: Yes, we were. What a coincident!

Comprehension Check!
What was Nicole doing last night? | What was Ken doing last night?

Role-Play
Using the above dialogue, roleplay with your partner using your own personal information.

Grammar Point 1 — Past Progressive: Wh-Questions (What)

Wh-questions (What)	Answers
What was I **doing**?	You **were taking** a walk.
What were you **doing**?	I **was watching** a soap opera.
What was he/she/it **doing**?	He/She/It **was taking** a nap.
What were we **doing**?	You **were attending** a party.
What were you **doing**?	We **were chatting** online.
What were they **doing**?	They **were going** out on a date.

Point!

mak**e** → mak**ing**   tak**e** → tak**ing**   hav**e** → hav**ing**
cha**t** → cha**tting**   se**t** → se**tting**   pu**t** → pu**tting**

Lesson 18 · 117

Grammar Point 2 — Past Progressive: Yes/No Questions

Yes/No Questions	Short Answers	
Was I **making** a phone call?	Yes, you **were**.	No, you **weren't**.
Were you **meeting** your boyfriend?	Yes, I **was**.	No, I **wasn't**.
Was he/she/it **taking** a nap?	Yes, he/she/it **was**.	No, he/she/it **wasn't**.
Were we **chatting** online?	Yes, you **were**.	No, you **weren't**.
Were you **having** a drink?	Yes, we **were**.	No, we **weren't**.
Were they **watching** a movie?	Yes, they **were**.	No, they **weren't**.

Practice
Practice the dialogue with a partner. See the example below.

Lily
at the park / walk her dog

Example

A: Where <u>was Lily</u> yesterday?
B: <u>She was at the park</u>.
A: What <u>was she</u> doing?
B: <u>She was walking her dog</u>.

1 Ned
at the mall / go out on a date

2 Joshua and Nicky
at the park / take a walk

3 Betty
at home / take a nap

4 Nicole
at the bar / have a drink

5 Kelly and Tom
at the movies / watch a movie

6 Ben
at the restaurant / meet his girlfriend

Pair Work

STUDENT A

Divide the class into pairs. One student will be **Student A**, and the other will be **Student B**. Referring to the sample dialogue below, form questions and answers using the information provided.

- 😀 : I have a question. Was <u>Jim watching a soap opera</u> at 6:00 last evening?
- 🙂 : No, <u>he</u> wasn't.
- 😀 : Then, what was <u>he</u> doing?
- 🙂 : <u>He</u> was <u>chatting online</u>.
- 😀 : What about at 7:00?
- 🙂 : <u>He</u> was <u>taking a walk</u>.

- 😀 : I have a question. Were <u>Jim and Ron watching a soap opera</u> at 6:00 last evening?
- 🙂 : No, <u>they</u> weren't.
- 😀 : Then, what were <u>they</u> doing?
- 🙂 : <u>They</u> were <u>chatting online</u>.
- 😀 : What about at 7:00?
- 🙂 : <u>They</u> were <u>taking a walk</u>.

1 Ask **Student B** questions about what the people in the chart did last evening and complete the table below.

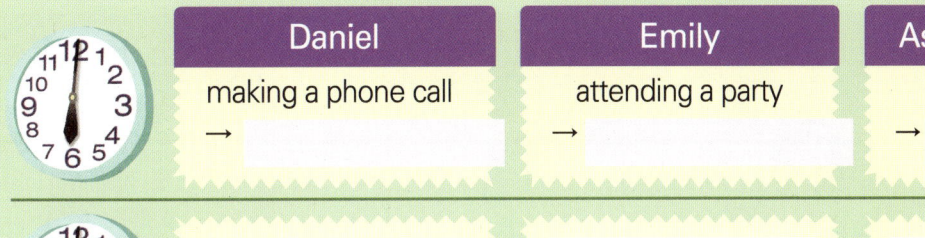

	Daniel	Emily	Ashley and Ethan
6:00	making a phone call →	attending a party →	having a drink →
7:00			

2 Answer **Student B**'s questions using the information below.

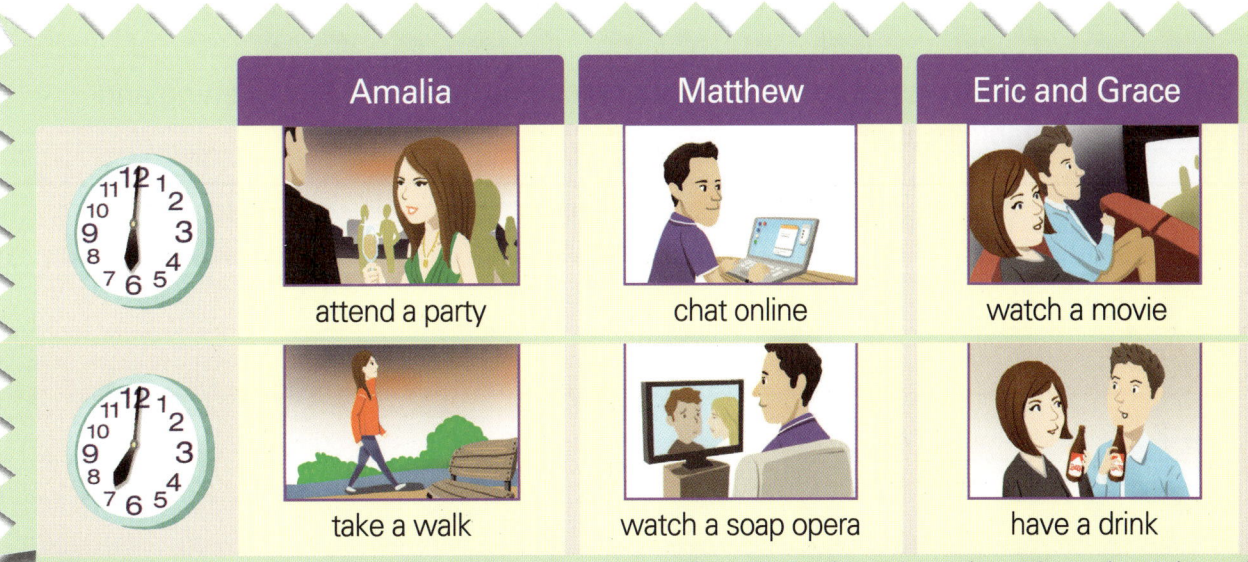

	Amalia	Matthew	Eric and Grace
6:00	attend a party	chat online	watch a movie
7:00	take a walk	watch a soap opera	have a drink

Pair Work

STUDENT B

Divide the class into pairs. One student will be **Student A**, and the other will be **Student B**. Referring to the sample dialogue below, form questions and answers using the information provided.

☺ : I have a question. Was <u>Jim watching a soap opera</u> at 6:00 last evening?
☺ : No, <u>he</u> wasn't.
☺ : Then, what was <u>he</u> doing?
☺ : <u>He</u> was <u>chatting online</u>.
☺ : What about at 7:00?
☺ : <u>He</u> was <u>taking a walk</u>.

☺ : I have a question. Were <u>Jim and Ron watching a soap opera</u> at 6:00 last evening?
☺ : No, <u>they</u> weren't.
☺ : Then, what were <u>they</u> doing?
☺ : <u>They</u> were <u>chatting online</u>.
☺ : What about at 7:00?
☺ : <u>They</u> were <u>taking a walk</u>.

1 Answer **Student A**'s questions using the information below.

	Daniel	Emily	Ashley and Ethan
6:00	go out on a date	meet her boyfriend	watch a movie
7:00	have a drink	walk her dog	take a nap

2 Ask **Student A** questions about what the people in the chart did last evening and complete the table below.

	Amalia	Matthew	Eric and Grace
6:00	walking her dog →	watching a movie →	grocery shopping →
7:00			

Pronunciation *Listen to the following sentences and repeat after them.*

1. She was watching a soap opera.
   He was watching a soap opera.

2. What were you doing at 9:00 last night?
   What were they doing at 9:00 last night?

3. She was having a drink with her co-workers.
   He was having a drink with his co-workers.

4. I was chatting online last night.
   You were chatting online last night.

5. What was she doing at 6 o'clock yesterday?
   What was he doing at 6 o'clock yesterday?

6. We were grocery shopping.
   She was grocery shopping.

Stretch Out!

Various Expressions You Can Use at a Bar

- Bottoms up!
- This drink is on me.
- Another round, please.
- Make mine a double.
- Put it on my tab.
- I'd like my drink straight / on the rocks.

Note

Note

Note